Winter Trails

ASPEN TO GLENWOOD

CROSS-COUNTRY SKIING
SNOWSHOEING · WINTER HIKING

WARREN OHLRICH

Published by People's Press
Woody Creek, CO · PeoplesPress.org

Published by People's Press

Post Office Box 70
Woody Creek, Colorado 81656
www.PeoplesPress.org

People's Press Mission

As the world becomes increasingly global, the need grows for community and for the cultivation of community identity through artistic insight. People's Press will search for books and the means to publish and distribute them to this purpose.

People's Press editorial board
Mirte Mallory
Nicole Beinstein Strait
George Stranahan

Library of Congress Control Number: 2009933697
ISBN: 978-0-9817810-2-0

Photos by Warren Ohlrich
Book design by Rainy Day Designs

Typeset in Meta, Bookman Old Style and Clarendon
Printed by Sheridan Books, Inc.

"There is a privacy about it which

no other season gives you...

In spring, summer and fall

people sort of have

an open season on each other;

only in the winter, in the country,

can you have longer,

quiet stretches when you can savor

belonging to yourself."

- Ruth Stout

❄

Table of Contents

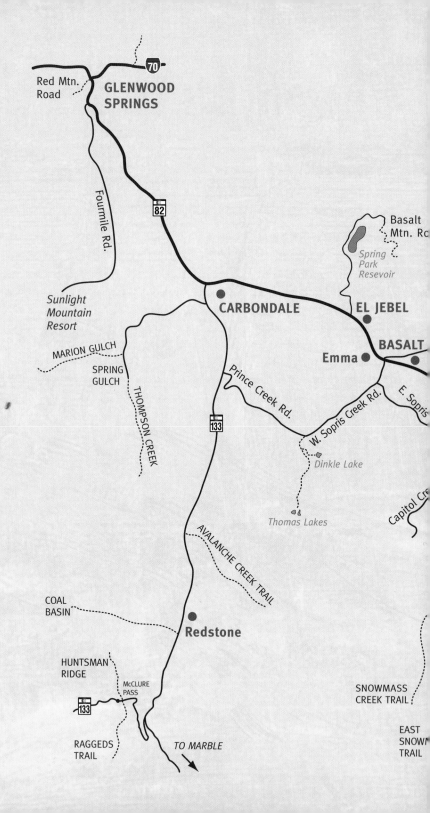

Valleywide Map

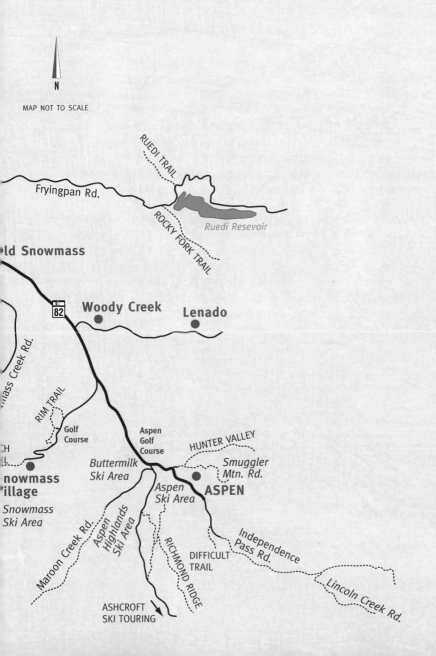

N

MAP NOT TO SCALE

RUEDI TRAIL

Fryingpan Rd.

ROCKY FORK TRAIL

Ruedi Resevoir

ld Snowmass

82 Woody Creek • Lenado •

Mass Creek Rd.

RIM TRAIL

Golf Course

Aspen Golf Course

HUNTER VALLEY

CH L

Buttermilk Ski Area

Smuggler Mtn. Rd.

nowmass illage •

Aspen Ski Area

ASPEN •

Snowmass Ski Area

Maroon Creek Rd.

Aspen Highlands Ski Area

RICHMOND RIDGE

Independence Pass Rd.

DIFFICULT TRAIL

Lincoln Creek Rd.

ASHCROFT SKI TOURING

Acknowledgements

THERE ARE MANY PEOPLE TO THANK FOR HELPING AND SUPPORTING ME WHILE I RESEARCHED AND GATHERED TOGETHER THE MATERIALS FOR THIS BOOK. I spend a lot of time out on the trails during the winter to gather all the information that is needed to compile a winter trails guide like this one and safety is always a major concern. Most of the routes were covered with at least one other person both for safety's sake, and to get someone else's perspective on the routes. My wife, Karen, not only supported the project but spent a lot of her time with me on the trails, both helping take pictures and providing a different point of view on what I was doing. Our good friend, Kristine Tracz, loves the backcountry and trails as much as we do and was a companion on many of the routes. Julian Martinez and Mariana took me to some trails that were new to me, and Les Gray and Peter Frey provided new insights as they accompanied me on routes that were not as familiar to me as I would have liked them to be.

Special thanks also to Austin Weiss, the Trails Coordinator for the City of Aspen, and to the Aspen/Snowmass Nordic Council for providing me with both much needed information and maps of the trail systems. Thanks to Ashcroft Ski Touring, the Mount Sopris Nordic Council and Sunlight Mountain Resort for use of the maps for their trail systems. Thanks also to Jen Moss for her extensive work on the design of this book.

The Aspen/Snowmass/Basalt/Carbondale/Glenwood area offers one of the country's most extensive networks of ski mountains, groomed cross-country tracks, and backcountry trails, all of which are available for cross-country skiers, snowshoers, hikers and other winter sports enthusiasts.

The valley's five ski mountains (Aspen Mountain, Aspen Highlands, Buttermilk, Snowmass, and Sunlight Mountain Resort) are available for "uphilling"—going up the mountain on skis, snowshoes or some kind of footwear for aerobic exercise. The Aspen/Snowmass Nordic Council trail system with hubs at the Aspen and Snowmass golf courses encompasses about 90 kilometers of groomed trails and is truly one of the finest free Nordic trail systems in the country. Ashcroft Ski Touring, a private organization, offers an additional 30 kilometers of groomed trails for skiing and snowshoeing at the end of the picturesque Castle Creek Valley. The Spring Gulch Trail System offers track skiing further down the valley near Carbondale in the scenic Jerome Park. Sunlight Mountain Resort has a cross-country trail system for the downvalley and Glenwood Springs area.

Other enjoyable routes for the cross-country skier, snowshoer or hiker include scores of scenic roads and trails which lead into the mountains and forests to areas not accessible by car. During the winter cross-country skiers, snowshoers and hikers can reach Maroon Lake, use Independence Pass Road, or enjoy the ridges that extend back from the tops of Aspen and Buttermilk mountains, or from McClure Pass. Many hiking trails, such as the Hunter Valley, Difficult, and Avalanche Creek trails also are available for winter touring.

Cross-country skiing has long been a popular sport and form of exercise in the valley, but snowshoeing and uphilling has become increasingly more popular in recent years. The history of the Aspen and Roaring Fork Valley area indicates that snowshoes were one of the primary means of winter travel and were instrumental in the settling of the Aspen area. In recent years, however, snowshoers have gotten into racing and snowshoeing just for fitness. Snowshoeing is essentially winter hiking, and requires far less technique than cross-country skiing. Most cross-country ski routes are also good for snowshoeing; however, many routes

are far better for snowshoeing because of the steepness or other factors which make them easier to snowshoe than to ski. Hiking some of the routes in boots, often with cleats attached, is another choice on trails that are packed out or have low snow cover. Many of the hikers take their dogs for exercise on the close-in packed-out trails.

TRAIL SYMBOLS

CROSS-COUNTRY SKIING　　　SNOWSHOEING　　　DOGS　　　HIKING

This winter trails guide lists and describes the many possibilities for both tourists and locals to enjoy the beauty of the area and to find routes for workouts or for getting away from the crowd. The guide clarifies which routes are best for skiing, snowshoeing, hiking, walking the dog, doing a workout, or whatever. A symbol (skis, snowshoes, boots, dog) for each trail indicates the appropriate use. Details are given for getting to trailheads, for

maps to use, distances, elevations, potential dangers from snow slides, and what to expect along the way. Under maps, three maps which are very specific for the trails in the Roaring Fork Valley are listed when applicable: *Aspen/Snowmass Outdoors, Basalt/ Carbondale Outdoors and Glenwood/Carbondale Outdoors.* TI # plus a number indicates the *Trails Illustrated* map which is appropriate for that trail.

For the more advanced cross-country skiers, skiing the backcountry can also be a rewarding experience. Using the hut systems is the safest and easiest way to enjoy the backcountry in the Aspen/Snowmass area. The 10th Mountain Division Hut Association manages a series of huts on a trail system which connects Aspen, Vail, and Leadville. The trails are routed around avalanche areas and the huts are well equipped for winter sojourns. For details on using this hut system, refer to the *10th Mountain Hut Book: A winter guide to Colorado's 10th Mountain and Summit hut systems near Aspen, Vail, Leadville and Breckenridge* by Warren Ohlrich.

✳

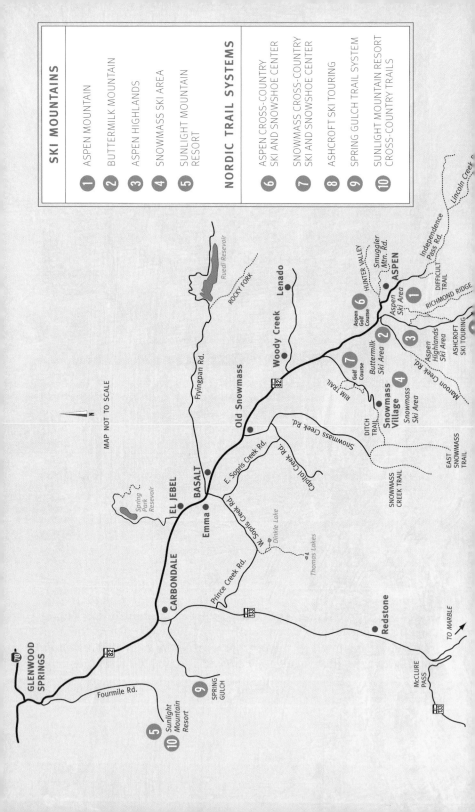

Snowshoeing and cross-country skiing had been a practical mode of moving around in the mountains during the Aspen winters since the mining days of the 1880s. Snowshoeing, however, didn't become a popular form of exercise in Aspen until a hundred years later, in the 1980s. A new form of competition, the Winter Mountain Man Triathlon, had come to the Beaver Creek Ski Area in Avon, Colorado. The events included cross-country skiing, snowshoeing, and speed skating. Of course, some of the local Aspen athletes (including the author) competed in this new event and took away many of the top prizes. Part of the training ritual for the Aspenites was to ascend Aspen Mountain early in the morning and then run back down to the bottom. As they ascended, they did have to put up with the expected comment from the downhill skiers—"You're going the wrong way." Most other people on the mountain did not even know what those "things" were on the snowshoers' feet. Soon, however, the winter triathlete snowshoers were joined by other uphill athletes who just wanted to get the exercise and the training effect of snowshoeing up Aspen Mountain. Others joined, just for the social aspect of it, and before long every morning, especially on weekends, snowshoers, cross-country skiers with skins, and other uphillers could be seen trudging up Aspen Mountain.

On March 19, 1988, America's Uphill, a race up Aspen Mountain, was born. The contestants ascended the mountain on snowshoes or skis with skins on the bottom. At first the race was for the competitive athlete, but very quickly it became a goal for many of the locals who just wanted to "do it." This uphill race propelled the uphill movement and soon snowshoers, skiers and hikers were seen regularly on all the ski mountains. The favorite became Buttermilk Mountain, where the trip to the top was shorter and it was possible to ascend any time of the day. A steady stream of uphillers, many with only hiking shoes on their feet, can be seen any time during the winter at Buttermilk.

Uphill races up the mountains are now regular winter events. All of the ski areas in the valley now hold uphill races, with Sunlight Mountain Resort extending their race into a 24-hour event.

❄

Aspen Mountain

MAP: Aspen/Snowmass Trail Map

DISTANCE: 2.3 miles with an elevation gain of 3,267 feet

ELEVATION: 7,945–11,212 feet

ACCESS: The route starts in Aspen at the base of Aspen Mountain next to the gondola building.

WEBSITE: www.aspensnowmass.com

Comments

Snowshoes are the ideal equipment to use when ascending Aspen Mountain because of the steepness of the route. However, some skiers like to use their telemark skis or alpine touring skis with skins, the reward being a ski down the mountain. Ski Company policy allows uphillers to download on the gondola free of charge. Because of potential collisions between downhill skiers and uphillers in the tight confines of Aspen Mountain, all uphillers are required to be at the top of Aspen Mountain by 9:00 a.m. Dogs are not allowed on the mountain. The race up Aspen Mountain— America's Uphill—is traditionally held in March.

Route

The usual route up the mountain follows the course of the America's Uphill race. Start up the Little Nell slope and cut over to the left. Follow the gully (Bingo Slot) to Spar Gulch and continue the long trek up the gulch, staying right at the intersection with Copper Bowl. Upon exiting Spar Gulch stay left in Tortilla Flats above the base of the Ajax Express lift, and go over the small knoll that takes you to Silver Dip. Follow Silver Dip under the gondola, continuing to the left to merge with 1&2 Leaf and Easy Chair which takes you back under the very top of the gondola to the Sundeck.

Buttermilk Mountain

MAP: Aspen/Snowmass Trail Map

DISTANCE: 1.5 miles one way

ELEVATION: 7,870–9,720 feet (East Summit), 7,870–9,900 feet (West Summit)

ACCESS: The base lodge at the Main Buttermilk Ski Area is located on the south side of Highway 82 three miles west of Aspen. Taking the bus (free from Aspen) or carpooling is encouraged to alleviate pollution and parking problems.

WEBSITE: www.aspensnowmass.com

Comments

Buttermilk Mountain has become the favorite stomping grounds for uphillers. Many Aspenites grab their snowshoes, skis or cleats at lunchtime and do a quick cruise up Buttermilk for a break. Visitors find Buttermilk the easiest and friendliest mountain for beginning and lower elevation uphilling. The views from the top of the surrounding valleys and peaks add an extra bonus to a successful completion of this uphill walk. The summit (East Summit) by the restaurant at the top of the mountain is the usual destination for most uphillers, but the West Buttermilk summit is only 200 feet higher in elevation and has the most spectacular views. For a longer trip you can also continue on the ridge going south from the West Buttermilk summit (see Route #25).

One of the advantages of going up Buttermilk is that you can make your trip any time during the day, and access to the base area is convenient by bus and car. All uphillers leaving from the base of Main Buttermilk must follow a designated route marked by orange disks. Uphillers can use any route going up West Buttermilk or East Buttermilk (Tiehack), but the only downloading is on the Summit Express lift. As always, uphillers are requested to stay to the side of the ski trails to avoid collisions with downhill skiers and snowboarders. Once at the top, you can either download on the Summit Express chairlift for free, or walk/run back down the designated route. Most prefer the walk back down—the chairlift ride down can often be a bit cold unless you have extra clothing. Dogs are not allowed on the mountain during the ski season. When the Winter X Games are at Buttermilk in January, uphillers are restricted to Tiehack and West Buttermilk.

Route

Start just above the base lodge, look for the sign for uphillers and follow the orange disks on the side of the trail to the left of the Summit Express. (The route may change from time to time, but will always be well marked.) Stay to the side of the trail and always be aware of skiers and snowboarders coming down the hill. Upon reaching the summit at the top of the Summit Express lift you can download, follow the marked route down, or continue up the ridge. To continue to the West Summit, take Tom's Thumb behind the restaurant up to the West Summit at the top of the West Buttermilk chairlift.

Top: Uphillers at Buttermilk with Pyramid Peak looming in the background
Bottom right: The start of the uphill route at Buttermilk

Aspen Highlands

MAP: Aspen/Snowmass Trail Map

DISTANCE: Varies, depending on the route taken; up to 7 miles roundtrip to Loge Peak.

ELEVATION: 8,040 feet (base)–9,975 feet (Merry-Go-Round)–11,675 feet (Loge Peak)

ACCESS: The easiest way to the slopes is taking the free ski bus to Aspen Highlands from Aspen or the shuttle from Buttermilk. Limited parking is available at the mountain; carpool if possible.

Comments

The ascent of Aspen Highlands on snowshoes, skis or other gear is a challenge, to say the least. To do the 3,635-foot vertical climb to the top of Loge Peak necessitates an early start—policy requires that to continue on past the Merry-Go-Round Restaurant at mid-mountain you must reach the restaurant by 9:00 a.m. However, the trip to mid-mountain can be made any time of the day using any route and is still a formidable elevation gain of over 1,900 feet. As on the other mountains, safety concerns dictate staying to the side of the trails, out of the way of the downhill skiers and snowboarders. Dogs are not allowed on the mountain, and downloading on the Exhibition Chair Lift from mid-mountain is free. Occasionally the mountain may be closed to uphillers due to avalanche control; a sign will be posted to that effect at the bottom of the chairlift.

Route

Start by the lodge in the base area at the bottom of the ski runs and use the trail map. The easiest route goes up Jerome Park, follows Park Avenue to Nugget and Riverside Drive. A less crowded route takes you up Thunderbowl and Golden Horn to T-Lazy-7 and Prospector, but more attention must be paid to the high-speed downhillers on this route. Downloading can only be done on the Exhibition Chair Lift.

Snowmass Ski Area

MAP: Aspen/Snowmass Trail Map

DISTANCE: Varies according to route selected

ELEVATION: 8,100–11,820 feet

ACCESS: The best access to Snowmass Village from Aspen is via the free skier shuttle buses. Parking is available at the Rodeo Lot for free with bus service to the slopes and free parking is available in the numbered lots after 1:00 p.m. Otherwise there is a fee for parking in the lots. Check the signs or call the Aspen Ski Company for the latest parking restrictions and bus service.

WEBSITE: www.aspensnowmass.com

The "Mother of All Ascensions" uphill race at Snowmass

Comments

The Snowmass Ski Area features a variety of terrain and routes for uphillers. Uphill traffic is allowed any time of the day and no specific routes are designated for uphillers. Downloading is allowed on most lifts except for the Elk Camp Meadows quad, the High Alpine double and the Sheer Bliss lift. What this all means is that a wide variety of routes with varying degrees of difficulty and of varying lengths are available. The on-mountain restaurants are obviously the most popular destinations. So take out the Aspen/ Snowmass Trail Map, pick a destination, avoid the black diamond runs, and head up the hill!

As on the other mountains, stay to the side of the slopes to avoid the downhill traffic. Be aware of snowcats and snowmobiles that may be encountered at any time working on the mountain. No dogs are allowed on the mountain during operating hours and no sledding is allowed. Wear headlamps at night.

Route

The popular starting points are at the base of Assay Hill, the base of Fanny Hill, and at the Village Mall. Since no designated route exists, choose your own way. Make good use of the Aspen/ Snowmass Trail Map.

SUGGESTED ROUTES TO THE RESTAURANTS: To Cafe Suzanne take Assay Hill and Funnel, or any route up Two Creeks. To Gwyn's High Alpine take Fanny Hill to Green Cabin to the restaurant (a steeper shortcut is up Coffee Pot). To the Ullrhof take Fanny Hill to Banzai and stay left. To the top of Sam's Knob take Fanny Hill to Dawdler to Scooper (or the steeper Hal's Hollow) to Lunchline and cut up to Banzai Ridge on either Max Park (easiest) or the run of your choice beforehand (depending on how steep you wish to go). The most direct route is Fanny Hill to Cabin to Banzai Ridge.

Sunlight Mountain Resort

MAP: Sunlight Mountain Resort Trail Map

DISTANCE: 3–5 miles roundtrip

ELEVATION: 8,170–9,900 feet

ACCESS: From 27th Street and Highway 82 in South Glenwood Springs turn west on 27th toward the river, cross the bridge, continue for 1.3 miles to the stop sign. Turn right toward Sunlight Mountain Resort onto Fourmile Road and drive 9.6 miles to the Sunlight Mountain Resort parking lot.

WEBSITE: www.sunlightmtn.com

Comments

The Sunlight Mountain Resort ski area (formerly Ski Sunlight) offers uphillers the opportunity to get a good workout by climbing to the summit of Compass Peak—a gain of over 1,700 feet in elevation from the base area. The climb to the top of the ski area can be done by snowshoers, skiers (with skins) or hikers (with cleats). Uphillers should be aware that they cannot download on the lift, so be prepared to walk or ski back down. There are no restrictions as to the time of day for uphillers to make their ascent, but it is requested that all uphillers stay close to the edge of the trails for safety's sake. Numerous routes can be taken, but the Ute run is the safest and roomiest. Ute can also be used to hook into the top of the cross-country system (see Route #10). Sunlight trail maps are available in the base area, or see the website.

Route

The favorite route up the mountain for uphillers is the 2.5-mile Ute run which follows the right (looking uphill) ski boundary of the ski area to the top. However, other beginner and intermediate trails can be combined to take shorter, but steeper, routes to the top. Snowshoers should have no trouble on the intermediate routes, but steeper intermediate trails may be harder to manage for skiers with skins. At any rate snowshoers, uphill skiers and hikers should stick to the edge of the trails and watch for downhill skiers.

Sunlight Mountain Resort

A number of Nordic trail systems are available to cross-country skiers in the Roaring Fork Valley between Aspen and Glenwood Springs.

THE ASPEN/SNOWMASS NORDIC TRAIL SYSTEM developed by the Aspen/Snowmass Nordic Council, is the largest and most popular system in the Roaring Fork Valley. The system contains about 90 kilometers of groomed trails. The eastern hub of the Aspen/Snowmass Nordic Trail System is the Aspen Cross-Country Center at the Aspen Golf Course, and the western hub is the Snowmass Cross-Country Center at the Snowmass Golf Course. The two hubs of the system are linked via the Owl Creek Trail. The machine-groomed tracks of the system contain set tracks for diagonal skiers and a packed path to the side of the tracks for skating skiers. Snowshoers are allowed on all the trails on the side of the packed path (not in the tracks), but no boots are allowed. Dogs and hikers are only allowed on a couple of designated loops at the golf courses and on the Marolt Open Space trails. No fee is charged for the use of the trails, but donations to the Nordic Council are encouraged to become a member of the Aspen/Snowmass Nordic Council. Maps of the system trails are available at the Aspen and Snowmass cross-country centers, or on the website. **(WWW.ASPENNORDIC.COM)**

ASHCROFT SKI TOURING is a private cross-country trail system located 11 miles from Aspen up Castle Creek Road in a spectacular backcountry setting, surrounded by peaks of the Elk Mountain Range. The groomed trails circle around and through the ghost town of Ashcroft, a mining town that rivaled Aspen in the late 1800s. This trail system also has its own restaurant, the Pine Creek Cookhouse, located in one of the most scenic settings of any restaurant in the country. A fee is charged for use of the trails, but the restaurant can also be accessed by a public, snow-covered road by skiers and snowshoers. **(WWW.SKIASHCROFT.COM)**

THE SPRING GULCH TRAIL SYSTEM near Carbondale is operated and maintained by the Mount Sopris Nordic Council. This popular downvalley system in Jerome Park charges no fees for use of the trails, but membership and/or donations are encouraged for frequent users of the trail system. No snowshoers or dogs are allowed on the trails, which are packed and set for both classic skiing and skate skiing. **(WWW.SPRINGGULCH.ORG)**

SUNLIGHT MOUNTAIN RESORT CROSS-COUNTRY TRAILS is located outside of Glenwood Springs adjacent to the Sunlight Mountain Resort Ski Area. The trails are only occasionally packed out for the skiers and snowshoers. No fees are charged and no cross-country center is available. The routes wind and climb mostly through the trees and offer an opportunity to climb all the way to the top of the Sunlight Mountain Resort Ski Area. **(WWW.SUNLIGHTMTN.COM)**

Aspen Cross-Country Ski and Snowshoe Center

ACCESS: By car, drive one mile west of Aspen on Highway 82 to the Aspen Cross-Country Center on the right. Parking is plentiful. By bus, take the local valley bus to the Truscott Place stop. By foot, you can ski or snowshoe across the Marolt Bridge on the west end of Aspen, staying right through the Marolt Property and follow the signs to cross Highway 82 to follow the trail to the Aspen Cross-Country Center.

WEBSITE: www.utemountaineer.com

Comments

The Aspen Cross-Country Center, the eastern hub of the Aspen/Snowmass Nordic Trail System, is located at the Aspen Golf Course by Highway 82 about one mile west of Aspen. The terrain is very flat, making this the ideal place for beginners to learn to cross-country ski. Cross-country skiers also come here to learn new skills, to practice and to get a good workout when travel time is limited. The center offers ski lessons, a retail shop, rentals, a lounge, lockers, snacks, and videos. The latest information on tours, lessons, rentals, etc. is available on the website. A restaurant is also on the premises.

The tracks at the golf course are linked with the Moore Trail, the High School Trail, the Marolt Trail, and with the Maroon Creek Club Trail, none of which is very difficult. The tracks are all set by pisten-bully snowcats, with packed lanes for skating set alongside the traditional tracks for diagonal striding. Snowshoers can use any of the trails, but should stay on the side to allow skiers to pass. The best snowshoeing is along Maroon Creek on the trail leading toward Buttermilk (see Route #20); this trail is generally ungroomed and provides a close-in backcountry experience. Dogs and walkers are not allowed on the tracks, except on Bernese Blvd., a multi-use trail which circles the Aspen Golf Course, and on the Marolt Trail on the southeast corner of Castle Creek Road and Highway 82. The Aspen Golf Course is generally the first area to be set after a new snowstorm. The elevation of the Aspen Cross-Country Center tracks ranges from 7,850–8,100 feet. For more information on the tracks visit the Cross-Country Center where details on the trails and maps are available.

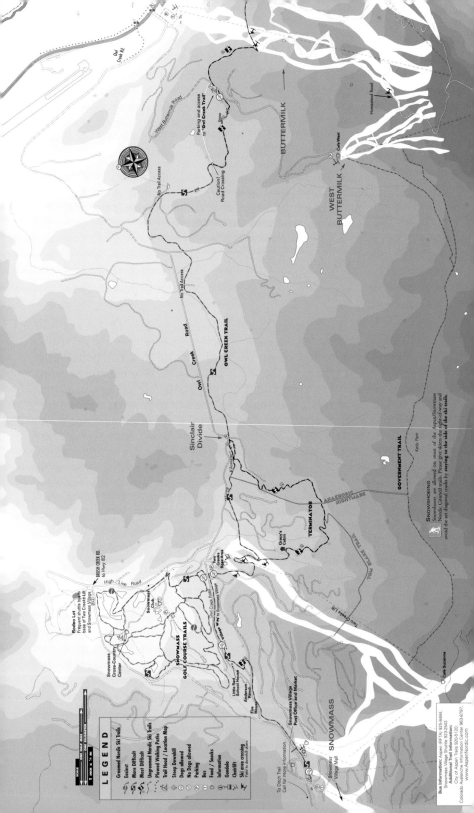

Snowmass Cross-Country Ski and Snowshoe Center

ACCESS: By car from Aspen or Snowmass, take Brush Creek Road toward Snowmass Village, continue through the roundabout and in 200 yards look for a left turn across from the Rodeo Parking Lot to the Snowmass Golf Course Clubhouse where the Cross-Country Center is located. By bus take any Snowmass Village bus to the Rodeo Lot, cross the street and walk a couple of hundred yards up Clubhouse Drive to the Cross-Country Center.

WEBSITE: www.utemountaineer.com

Comments

The cross-country tracks in the Snowmass Village area spread out from the Snowmass Cross-Country Center, the western hub of the Aspen/Snowmass Nordic Council Trail System. The Center, located at the Snowmass Golf Course Clubhouse across from the Rodeo Lot, has a retail shop, snack bar, and lounge, and offers lessons, rentals, tours, picnic lunches, and occasional special events. Food is available at the Two Creeks base area.

Both snowshoers and skiers can find some pleasant touring around the golf course. Dogs and hikers are only allowed on Labrador Lane, a multi-use trail. In addition to the tracks set on the golf course, there are also trails set on the south side of Owl Creek Road. The Terminator Loop, which lies mostly in the woods and open meadows at the base of Burnt Mountain and loops around the Two Creeks development, is a fine, pleasant trail for advanced cross-country skiers, and an excellent snowshoe tour. The Owl Creek Trail (see Route #27), heads east from the Two Creeks Ski Area, crosses the Buttermilk Ski Area, and hooks up with the Aspen Cross-Country Center tracks.

The tracks in the Snowmass Village area vary in difficulty from beginner to advanced and range in elevation from 8,000–8,600 feet. For more information on the tracks, visit the Cross-Country Center where details on the trails and maps are available.

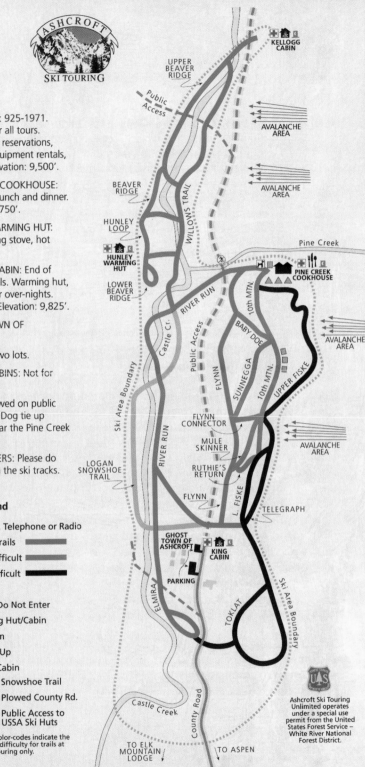

Facilities

KING CABIN: 925-1971.
Trail head for all tours.
Information, reservations,
complete equipment rentals,
ski shop. Elevation: 9,500'.

PINE CREEK COOKHOUSE:
925-1044. Lunch and dinner.
Elevation: 9,750'.

HUNLEY WARMING HUT:
Woodburning stove, hot
drinks.

KELLOGG CABIN: End of
Ashcroft trails. Warming hut,
also used for over-nights.
Hot drinks. Elevation: 9,825'.

**GHOST TOWN OF
ASHCROFT**

PARKING: Two lots.

PRIVATE CABINS: Not for
public use.

DOGS: Allowed on public
access only. Dog tie up
available near the Pine Creek
Cookhouse.

SNOWSHOERS: Please do
not walk on the ski tracks.

Map Legend

✚ First Aid, Telephone or Radio
▬ Easiest Trails ▬▬▬
▨ More Difficult ▬▬▬
◆ Most Difficult ▬▬▬
△ Danger
⊛ Closed. Do Not Enter
🏠 Warming Hut/Cabin
🚻 Restroom
🐕 Dog Tie Up
▢ Private Cabin
▬▬▬ Snowshoe Trail
▬▬▬ Plowed County Rd.
▬ ▬ ▬ Public Access to
USSA Ski Huts

Symbols and color-codes indicate the
relative skiing difficulty for trails at
Ashcroft Ski Touring only.

Ashcroft Ski Touring
Unlimited operates
under a special use
permit from the United
States Forest Service –
White River National
Forest District.

Ashcroft Ski Touring

ACCESS: Take Highway 82 west from Aspen one-half mile to the roundabout and exit onto Castle Creek Road toward the hospital and Ashcroft. Go 11 miles up the road to parking on the left for Ashcroft.

WEBSITE: www.skiashcroft.com

Comments

Ashcroft Ski Touring is nestled in the end of Castle Creek Valley in the White River National Forest. The nearby 14,000-foot peaks and the mountains at the end of the valley provide the backdrop, and the remaining buildings of the historic ghost town of Ashcroft give the valley and the ski touring trails a character all of its own. The buildings of the ghost town of Ashcroft are located just across from Nordic center.

Ashcroft, originally a silver mining town, sprang up about the same time as Aspen in 1879. Due to some initial good strikes and the accessibility over Cottonwood and Taylor passes, Ashcroft got the jump on Aspen and became a thriving mining town. Horace Tabor and Baby Doe were occasional visitors to Ashcroft after Tabor purchased the Tam O'Shanter mines in 1881. When the two railroads came to Aspen, most of the miners left Ashcroft and moved to Aspen. By the late 1880s, Ashcroft was all but forgotten. In the late 1930s, Castle Creek Valley and the Ashcroft area were considered for the region's first major ski area, a distinction that Aspen eventually claimed. Later, Ashcroft and Toklat became the home of Stuart Mace's sled dog teams for many years. Eventually the cross-country ski trails became the focal point of this resort area. Ashcroft is generally thought to have been named after T.E. Ashcraft, one of the town's original prospectors. However, it may have been named for the many ash trees in the croft (an Anglo-Saxon word for a small enclosed field).

Ashcroft Ski Touring has about 35 kilometers of cross-country and snowshoe trails. The trails vary from the easy flat trails on the valley floor to the advanced trails in the trees on the side of the valley. The elevation range for trails at Ashcroft Ski Touring is from 9,500–9,800 feet. Ashcroft Ski Touring is a self-sustaining operation that charges a fee for the use of the trails. Lessons and ski and snowshoe rentals are available at the Nordic center. All the trails are groomed daily with either a snowcat for the main trails, or a snowmobile for the narrower trails. Snowshoeing is allowed on all trails except on River Run along Castle Creek, due to its narrowness. The Logan Snowshoe Trail parallels River Run and is for snowshoers only. Snowshoeing is allowed and encouraged in the 12-acre ghost town area for no fee.

Where possible, the trails are groomed for both diagonal striding and skating. The Willows trail (south of Beaver Ridge) and the road to Kellogg Cabin are often closed because of avalanche danger. The road going through the area is open to the public for free skiing and snowshoeing and is used to access the world-famous Pine Creek Cookhouse, some of the Braun huts and the Pearl Pass area.

The Pine Creek Cookhouse, named after Pine Creek which flows nearby to the south, is located about 1.5 miles south of the Nordic center, and is nestled against the side of the valley. The views of the mountains at the end of the valley are breathtaking, making this an ideal spot for a gourmet lunch or dinner. You can ski in just for lunch, or come on a romantic sleigh ride or guided ski tour by lantern for dinner. Reservations are required.

Other facilities in the Ashcroft Ski Touring system include the historic Kellogg Cabin and Hunley Warming Hut.

Ashcroft Ski Touring Trails

FLYNN is the most used route between King Cabin and the Pine Creek Cookhouse. It also is a part of the long beginner trail that loops through the area. The trail was named after Tom Flynn, who in the late 1930s created interest for skiing in the Castle Creek Valley, bringing in Billy Fiske, Ted Ryan, and others.

WILLOWS makes a good continuation of the long beginner's route which begins with Flynn, and is the best route to use to get to the Kellogg Cabin. The Hunley Warming Hut is located just off this trail.

RIVER RUN, a narrow route along Castle Creek, lives up to its reputation as one of the most beautiful of all the trails in the valley. River Run can be reached from the ghost town of Ashcroft, but most people take the trail from south to north since it slopes gradually downhill in this direction. The southern access is by the Pine Creek Cookhouse.

10TH MOUNTAIN TRAIL is the central trail in the group of trails on the west side of the valley between King Cabin and the Pine Creek Cookhouse. This trail is almost entirely in the aspen trees. The changing terrain and the winding trail make 10th Mountain a more interesting, although more difficult route to the Pine Creek Cookhouse than Flynn.

BEAVER RIDGE is a good return route from the Kellogg Cabin and accesses the Hunley Warming Hut. Beaver Ridge is reached by the Willows Trail and is easier when skied from south to north. Several climbs and descents makes this a somewhat challenging, although interesting, trail along the southeastern slopes of Ashcroft Ski Touring.

FISKE AND TELEGRAPH HILL, the most difficult trails in the cross-country ski area, involve some steep hills along the western boundary of Ashcroft Ski Touring. These slopes are often closed because of unsafe avalanche conditions. When open they offer the better skier a good challenge on tackling hills in the beautiful groves of aspen and spruce. Fiske is named after Billy Fiske, an Olympic bobsledder and later member of the 10th Mountain Division. He was one of the original promoters of skiing in the Aspen area, especially in the Castle Creek Valley.

ELMIRA runs through the open area by the remaining buildings of the ghost town of Ashcroft and can either be combined with the more difficult gladed Toklat Loop for a loop, or it makes a great beginner's trip from the Nordic center through the ghost town into the open area by Castle Creek.

LEFT: Taking the 10th Mountain Trail through the aspen trees
RIGHT: The Pine Creek Cookhouse at Ashcroft

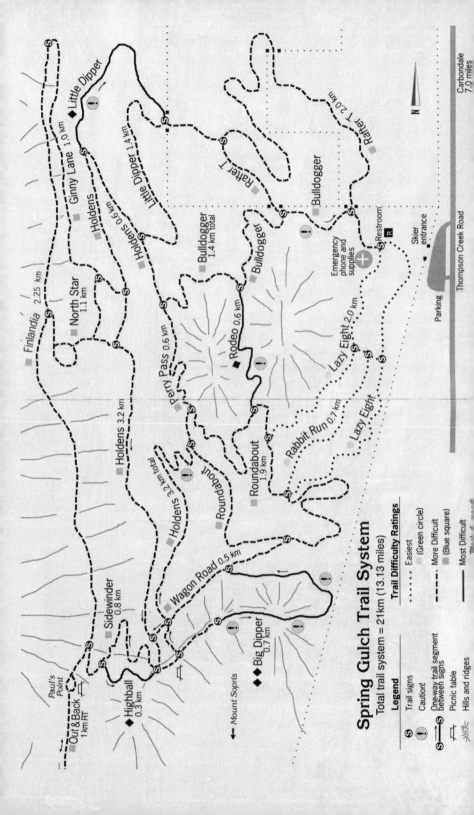

Spring Gulch Trail System

Total trail system = 21km (13.13 miles)

Legend

Ⓢ Trail signs

! Caution!

Ⓢ–Ⓢ One-way trail segment between signs

⌂ Picnic table

🏔 Hills and ridges

Trail Difficulty Ratings

· · · · · · · Easiest (Green circle)

– – – – – More Difficult (Blue square)

▬▬▬▬ Most Difficult

Little Dipper

Ginny Lane 1.0 km

Holdens

Holdens 0.6 km

Little Dipper 1.4 km

Finlandia 2.25 km

North Star 1.1 km

Holdens 3.2 km

Perry Pass 0.6 km

Bulldogger 1.4 km total

Bulldogger

Bulldogger

Rodeo 0.6 km

Rafter T 2.0 km

Rafter T

Bulldogger

Emergency phone and supplies

Restroom R

Skier entrance

Lazy Eight 2.0 km

Lazy Eight

Rabbit Run 0.7 km

Roundabout 1.9 km

Roundabout

Holdens 3.2 km total

Sidewinder 0.8 km

Paul's Point

Out & Back 1 km RT

Highball 0.3 km

Wagon Road 0.5 km

Big Dipper 0.7 km

Mount Sopris

Parking

Thompson Creek Road

Carbondale 7.0 miles

N

Spring Gulch Trail System

ACCESS: Take Highway 133 to the light at Main Street in Carbondale (by the 7-11 store) and turn west on County Road 108 (Thompson Creek Road). Follow Thompson Creek Road 7 miles to the Spring Gulch Trail System parking area on the right at the end of the plowed road.

WEBSITE: www.springgulch.org

Comments

The Spring Gulch Trail System located 7 miles west of Carbondale on Thompson Creek Road in Jerome Park—a beautiful rural valley which is somewhat isolated from the development taking place in nearby areas—is maintained and operated by the Mount Sopris Nordic Council, a community-based non-profit organization. No fees are charged for the use of these trails, but membership in the Mount Sopris Nordic Council is encouraged for anyone who may use the trails on a regular basis. These tracks are for cross-country skiers only and no dogs are allowed on the trail system. Snowshoers venturing into this valley may want to use Marion Gulch (see Route #45) which is located just down the road, or the continuation of Thompson Creek Road (see Route #47). A sledding hill for the kids is located just across the road from Spring Gulch.

The 21 kilometers of trails meander through scrub growth and trees, along the valley floor, and up onto the side of the valley, giving great views of Mount Sopris and other natural landmarks in the area. The elevation range is from 7,750–8,300 feet. All levels of skiers can find trails in this system that will suit their abilities. For those interested in racing, every winter a race for both diagonal striders and skaters is held on the trail system.

The trails are groomed and maintained on a regular basis, with both a packed lane and tracks being set for both skaters and striders. One of the primary goals of this trail system is to preserve the natural setting, which has been done extremely well. No services other than a restroom are provided, and an emergency phone is available. A large trail map is posted at the beginning of the system and individual trail maps are also available for users.

Spring Gulch Trails

The trail system is set up in such a manner that it is possible to make up dozens of different routes, combining the trails in a variety of ways. Some of the more popular routes and tours are suggested below.

LAZY EIGHT/RABBIT RUN which starts by the entrance, is a flat beginner's run that is good for easy striding or skating, or for warming up. The Lazy Eight and Rabbit Run can be combined in a number of different ways, going in either direction.

RAFTER T/BULLDOGGER LOOP starts by the restroom. Rafter T takes off through the brush and open country to the far north side of the ski trail system. This peaceful tour is best done in a counterclockwise direction if you want to form a loop with Bulldogger.

RAFTER T/LITTLE DIPPER/HOLDENS/GINNY LANE/FINLANDIA/PAUL'S POINT/ HIGHBALL/WAGON ROAD/ROUNDABOUT/LAZY EIGHT (SPRING GULCH LOOP) follows the perimeter of the trail system, avoiding the one-way advanced Little Dipper, and the steep hills on the expert Big Dipper. This grand tour of the Spring Gulch Trail System will give you a good workout and overview of the trail system and the valley in which it's located.

HOLDENS LOOP, an easy intermediate loop, winds through the center of the trail system and forms a great 4.5-mile tour with easy rolling hills and curves. Follow upper Lazy Eight/Roundabout/ Perry Pass/Holdens/Wagon Road/Lazy Eight/Roundabout to Lazy Eight, where a right takes you back to the beginning.

BIG/LITTLE DIPPER TOUR, for the advanced skier who likes the hills and some excitement, involves a bit of climbing and some fast downhills. Take Lazy Eight/Roundabout/Wagon Road/Holdens/ Sidewinder/Highball/Big Dipper then back to Wagon Road/ Holdens/Perry Pass/Holdens/Little Dipper/Rafter T/Bulldogger to start.

Top: Mount Sopris towering over the Spring Gulch trails

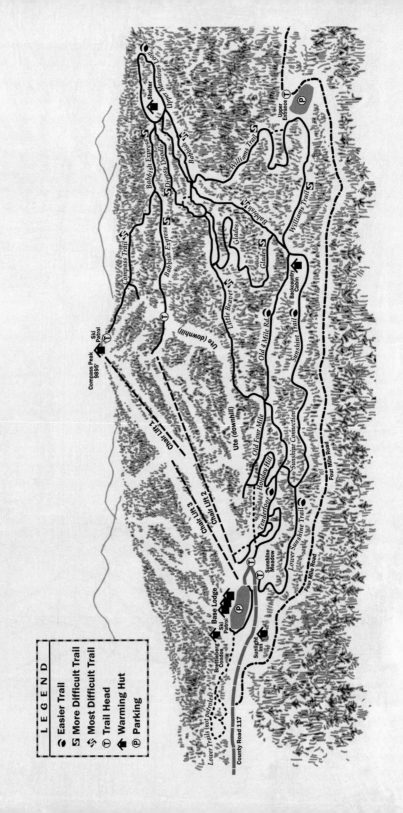

Sunlight Mountain Resort Cross-Country Trails

10

ACCESS: From 27th Street and Highway 82 in South Glenwood Springs turn west on 27th toward the river, cross the bridge, continue for 1.3 miles to the stop sign. Turn right toward Sunlight Mountain Resort onto Fourmile Road and drive 9.6 miles to the Sunlight Mountain Resort parking lot . At the beginning of the parking lot is a packed road going uphill to the west. This is your starting point. (You can also start on the ski slope by the fence above the base facility and traverse over.) For a parking area higher up that allows you to avoid the initial long uphill climb from the Sunlight parking lot, turn off on Fourmile Road just before the ski area and drive 2.2 miles to parking on the left.

WEBSITE: www.sunlightmtn.com

Comments

Sunlight Mountain Resort offers a variety of trails for cross-country skiing and snowshoeing. The trail system winds through woods of large old aspen and spruce/fir in and around Babish Gulch, a high valley between the ski area (located on Compass Peak) and Williams Peak. Some packed grooming is done, but no tracks are set. Maintenance of the trails varies from year to year. A small backcountry cabin near the beginning of the tracks can be rented for overnight use (call Sunlight Mountain Resort for reservations). Another small ski shelter with a stove and firewood for emergencies lies further up the trails. From the top of the system you have good views of Sunlight, Williams, and Compass peaks. There is a choice of many side routes of varying degrees of difficulty off the main groomed track; you can even climb to the summit of Compass Peak, the top of the ski area. The elevation range is 8,150–9,740 feet. Take along your sense of adventure, allow time, and enjoy!

Sunlight Mountain Trails

From the Sunlight Mountain Resort parking lot climb past the Sunlight Stables building on the packed road (Old Fourmile Road—occasionally snowmobiles can be encountered on this road section, especially on weekends). On the right are some off-the-road tracks you can follow if you wish towards the backcountry cabin. Three-quarters of a mile up the Old Fourmile Road lies the backcountry cabin on the right. At this point you have a choice whether to continue on the packed Williams Trail straight ahead or to go left uphill off the beaten track on an unpacked track for .7 miles through the aspen and open areas of Babbish Gulch to the intersection with the Williams Trail.

For the longer route, follow the packed Williams Trail past the cabin to where the road is blocked off (going straight ahead takes you to the parking lot on Fourmile Road). Turn left uphill on the groomed track. The route from here is a steady uphill through beautiful woods with occasional views of the valley and ski area. After the Babbish Trail joins the Williams Trail it is just another half mile to a small, half-buried shelter at 8,970 feet, just over 2 miles from the backcountry cabin and start of the Williams Trail.

Entrance to the Sunlight Cross-Country Trails on Old Fourmile Road

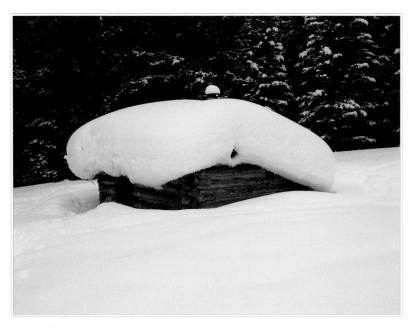

The half-buried shelter on the Williams Trail at Sunlight

From the shelter you have a number of choices. You can retreat and call it a day, or add a loop from the shelter to the west (Upper Meadows Loop), a not too difficult but scenic loop that starts just before the shelter and hooks up with the Williams Trail just beyond the shelter. You can also cross over to the Glades on the other side of the small gully from the shelter and work your way down, sometimes through untracked snow. Or you can continue ahead on Babbish Express to the ski slopes .7 miles from the shelter.

At the ski slopes you can either double back or climb up the edge of the Ute ski slope. Either take an early cutoff to the right, or keep heading up the slope. In .6 miles, after gaining 600 feet to elevation 9,740, just short of the Compass Peak summit, you come to the Compass cross-country trail going down to the right (just beyond the small wedding chapel). You can follow the sometimes packed track down to the right, or stay to the side in the untracked snow, to continue down to the area of the shelter. From here a good route down is the sometimes packed Dipsy-Doodle Trail which descends to the right (east) of Babbish Gulch. Eventually you hook up with Old Fourmile Road to return to the parking lot.

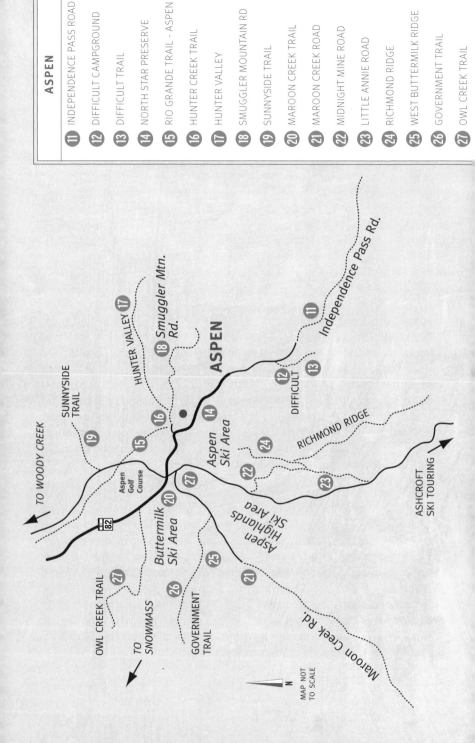

ASPEN

11 INDEPENDENCE PASS ROAD
12 DIFFICULT CAMPGROUND
13 DIFFICULT TRAIL
14 NORTH STAR PRESERVE
15 RIO GRANDE TRAIL - ASPEN
16 HUNTER CREEK TRAIL
17 HUNTER VALLEY
18 SMUGGLER MOUNTAIN RD
19 SUNNYSIDE TRAIL
20 MAROON CREEK TRAIL
21 MAROON CREEK ROAD
22 MIDNIGHT MINE ROAD
23 LITTLE ANNIE ROAD
24 RICHMOND RIDGE
25 WEST BUTTERMILK RIDGE
26 GOVERNMENT TRAIL
27 OWL CREEK TRAIL

A spen is a virtual hub for cross-country and snowshoeing possibilities, with routes in every direction from the town. You can head up Independence Pass Road, into Hunter Valley, onto the golf course, up Maroon Creek Road or Castle Creek Road, or over to the Buttermilk Ski Area.

Many snow-covered roads, trails, and ridges provide opportunities for both skiers and snowshoers to "get away from it all." The roads (Independence Pass, Smuggler Mountain, Maroon Creek, Midnight Mine and Little Annie) all provide snow-covered, wide pathways for both snowshoers and cross-country skiers to follow. Some of these also have snowmobile traffic which help pack out the roads. The trails (Hunter Creek, Hunter Valley, Difficult, Government, Owl Creek) lead through more pristine settings, and Richmond Ridge and West Buttermilk Ridge provide high altitude backcountry experiences. The best routes for hikers and dogs are Independence Pass Road, Difficult Campground, Rio Grande Trail, Hunter Creek Trail, Smuggler Mountain Road, Sunnyside Trail and Maroon Creek Road.

Independence Pass Road

MAPS: Aspen/Snowmass Outdoors, TI #127

DISTANCE: Varies. 8.5 miles (to Lincoln Creek Road and back)

ELEVATION: 8,600–9,820 feet (at Lincoln Creek Road)

ACCESS: Drive southeast from Aspen on Highway 82 until you reach the end of the plowed road (just over 5 miles from Aspen). There is ample parking here at the snow closure gate.

Comments

Every winter Highway 82 closes for the season southeast of Aspen due to the heavy winter snows and the difficulty in keeping the road open to Independence Pass (elevation 12,095 feet). The road beyond the snow closure gate offers an excellent opportunity for cross-country skiers, snowshoers and hikers to enjoy the majesty of the upper Roaring Fork Valley without having to concern themselves about traffic. Snowmobilers also use the road; dogs are allowed. The gentle and wide route is well packed down by snowmobiles all the way to the ghost town of Independence (mile marker 57), beyond which there is significant avalanche danger. Generally, most skiers and snowshoers don't go any farther than Lincoln Creek Road (just past mile marker 51). Miles are marked by green mile markers (which indicate the distance from Interstate 70 in Glenwood Springs). The route starts at mile marker 47.

LEFT: The snow closure gate on Independence Pass Road
RIGHT: Independence Pass Road at a narrow point

Route

This popular route starts at the snow closure gate at mile marker 47. It is impossible to get lost—all you have to do is to follow the road. The road is packed down by snowmobilers, skiers, snowshoers and walkers, making it a little chopped up for skate skiing. As you head up the road from the gate, you will be above the Roaring Fork River which runs through the valley below to the right; the scenery is dominated by the snow-covered peaks forming the valley walls. No severe avalanche danger exists before Lincoln Creek Road, but rocks often come down onto the road, especially along the initial part of this route.

The first couple of miles ascend very gradually uphill; just before mile marker 49 the road gets narrower as it cuts into the side of the valley wall above the Roaring Fork River. This series of curves is always very tight for cars in the summer, but for the cross-country skier or snowshoer there is plenty of room.

Since the road is on the north side of the valley, it catches a lot of sun, making the trip very pleasant on a sunny day. Be sure to enjoy the many good places to stop and picnic, with good rocks for sitting or climbing on. With luck, at some spots you may even be able to get down to the river.

Past mile marker 49 the road levels a bit as you pass Weller Campground. Just before mile marker 50 you will be going through the beautiful narrow part of the valley, right alongside the Roaring Fork River. Rock walls rise steeply up on the left, and just past mile 50 you come to the Grottos. Lincoln Creek Road is about 300 yards beyond mile 51 on the right.

If you still have time, you can head about 2 miles up Lincoln Creek Road before hitting areas of severe avalanche danger. The first part is downhill, before the steady uphill. The road follows the creek, passing through beautiful wooded and open areas.

For the energetic skier or snowshoer wishing to go past Lincoln Creek Road on Independence Pass Road, you can still travel another 6 miles to the ghost town of Independence before having to turn back because of avalanche danger. For safety's sake don't travel alone past Lincoln Creek Road, since this stretch is seldom used by others and some slide danger is present.

Difficult Campground

MAPS: Aspen/Snowmass Outdoors, TI #127

DISTANCE: 1–2 mile; the distance can be extended by crisscrossing around throughout the campground area

ELEVATION: 8,150 feet

ACCESS: Take Highway 82 southeast from Aspen for 3.5 miles to just beyond mile marker 45. There will be parking on the right alongside the road just before the White River National Forest sign. The road leading down to the right comes to a gate which is the entrance to the campground.

Comments

Difficult Campground, located off Independence Pass Road, is ideally located for a quick trip from Aspen into the unspoiled outdoors of the upper Roaring Fork Valley. The campground is situated in the trees alongside the Roaring Fork River on the old wagon trail to Independence Pass. This area is popular with dog owners for walking their dogs, and for Aspenites who wish to take a break during the day not far from town. There are no set tracks—the trail is packed down by walkers, snowshoers, and skiers. The harder Difficult Trail (see Route #13) also begins here at the campground.

Route

Follow the road through the gate into the campground. At the Day Use Area the Difficult Trail goes out of the end of the parking lot on the right toward the river. Or you can continue straight ahead on the main campground road to wander through the camp area. The terrain is flat with side routes on the right leading to the Roaring Fork River. This all is a good touring area, with some pleasant easy striding. You can explore and break you own trail, if you wish, or follow trails packed by other skiers and walkers. History buffs should note that the wagon trail from Leadville passed through here in the 1880s.

Difficult Trail

MAPS: Aspen/Snowmass Outdoors, TI #127

DISTANCE: 2–4 miles

ELEVATION: 8,150–9,000 feet

ACCESS: Follow the directions given above to Difficult Campground. At the Day Use Area parking area on the right the Difficult Trail exits the parking area on the left towards the river.

Comments

This heavily wooded trail is a good trip for the adventurous, both in summer and in winter. The trail becomes narrow, steep, and difficult to ski—snowshoeing is the preferred mode. If you take your time and enjoy the scenery, what is a relatively short trip can become an enjoyable half-day or longer excursion. Avalanche danger becomes severe farther up the trail, so it is wise not to continue past the area where the route starts cutting into the steep rocky walls. The only tracks to be found on this trail are those of other skiers and snowshoers, and you may have to break your own trail.

Route

Follow the trail signs to the Roaring Fork River going left to a bridge over the river. Across the bridge go right and head up the bank on the left which will bring you onto a broad sagebrush plateau with scrub oak. The trail (usually packed by others, but not always) continues off to the east across this old river terrace, goes through some scrub trees, then comes to Difficult Creek. From here, the trail ascends steeply uphill alongside the creek through the pine and fir forest. Snowshoers can easily continue, but most skiers turn around here. If you're a good skier ready for some adventure, continue up into the trees along the creek. The trail is wooded and relatively narrow in most places. As the trail starts bending away from the creek, it levels off somewhat up through the wooded area, then ascends more steeply as you approach the valley wall. It's best not to go any farther because of avalanche danger—from here the trail cuts into steep banks on the side of the valley.

North Star Preserve

MAP: Nordic Council map

DISTANCE: A little over 1.5 miles

ELEVATION: 8,000 feet

ACCESS: Drive about 1.5 miles east of Aspen on Highway 82 to parking on the right.

Comments

Situated 1.5 miles east of Aspen just off Highway 82, the 175-acre North Star Preserve lies in a large open area intersected by the Roaring Fork River. The loop in the preserve gives you outstanding views toward Independence Pass and of the mountains surrounding the upper end of the Roaring Fork Valley. This loop is a part of the Nordic Council Trail System, so tracks are set for the cross-country skiers. Snowshoeing is allowed on the sides of the trail, but skiing is the preferred and more enjoyable mode. The loop is relatively flat and much of it goes alongside the Roaring Fork River. The loop is also an ideal training ground for cross-country skiers on skating skis. Dogs are prohibited on this loop because of wildlife concerns.

Route

From the parking area on Highway 82 follow the set tracks in either direction as they loop around in the North Star Nature Preserve adjacent to the Roaring Fork River. The main loop is a little over 1.5 miles, but it is possible to make shorter loop and combine these with the main loop for any distance that is needed. It's impossible to get lost—everything is in sight from any part of the loop.

Rio Grande Trail – Aspen

MAPS: Aspen/Snowmass Outdoors, Basalt/Carbondale Outdoors

DISTANCE: Post office to Stein Park (Cemetery Lane) 1.8 miles, Stein Park to McLain Flats Road 4.2 miles, McLain Flats Road to Woody Creek Road 1.7 miles (see Route #24 for continuation downvalley)

ELEVATION: Aspen Post Office 7,900 feet, Stein Park 7,735 feet, McLain Flats Road 7,540 feet, Woody Creek Road 7,365 feet

ACCESS: The eastern end of the Rio Grande Trail starts by the Aspen Post Office. From the Hotel Jerome, go north on Mill Street to the second left (Puppy Smith Street). The trail entrance is down Puppy Smith, 100 feet on the right just across from the post office. The trail can also be accessed at Stein Park by taking Cemetery Lane (first stoplight west of town) north one mile to where the trail crosses at the Roaring Fork River. There is a parking lot on the left just past the bridge. This access can also be reached by taking the free Snowbunny Bus from Rubey Park in Aspen. The Woody Creek access is just west of the Woody Creek Tavern on McLain Flats Road.

Comments

The most accessible and popular of all the trails in the Aspen area, the Rio Grande Trail follows the old Denver and Rio Grande Railroad bed along the Roaring Fork River. In the winter it is possible to follow this trail along the old scenic railroad corridor all the way from the post office in Aspen to Rock Bottom Ranch between Basalt and Carbondale, a distance of about 23 miles. Since much of the trail runs through the open valley, the snow on the Rio Grande Trail tends to deteriorate quickly when the weather is warm. Tracks are set on most of the trail when snow cover is adequate. The Rio Grande Trail is a multi-use trail. Hikers and dogs are allowed on the trail, but dogs must be on a leash.

Route

From the post office, the trail leads over two bridges—the first goes over the Roaring Fork River, the second over Hunter Creek. The trail continues along the right (north) side of the Roaring Fork River the rest of the way. To the west of Cemetery Lane, the next mile or so is very scenic as the trail follows the river in a small canyon-like setting. At one point on the right, the water flows down the rocks, creating some very interesting ice formations. You will see little sign of civilization until you get close to the Airport Business Center which is across the river on the left.

Past the Airport Business Center are some great views of the Roaring Fork Valley and the Elk Mountain Range. The river runs below in a small gorge. Across the valley you can see all of the four downhill ski areas: Aspen Mountain, Aspen Highlands, Buttermilk, and Snowmass. When snow levels are low, this part of the trail sometimes isn't in good shape because of its exposure to the sun. The trail continues high above the river with several road crossings before reaching Woody Creek.

A reminder of the railroad history along the Rio Grande Trail

Hunter Creek Trail

MAPS: Aspen/Snowmass Outdoors, TI #127

DISTANCE: 2 miles roundtrip to the Benedict Bridge

ELEVATION: 7,900–8,400 feet

ACCESS: By foot or by car: go north on Mill Street from Main Street (by Hotel Jerome), cross the bridge over the Roaring Fork, bear left on Red Mountain Road, then take the next right onto Lone Pine Road. The signed trailhead is about 100 yards on the left between the Hunter Longhouse and the Hunter Creek Condominiums (one-half mile from the center of town). By bus: take the Hunter Creek Bus and get off at the Hunter Creek Condominiums.

Comments

One of the most accessible winter trails from Aspen, the Hunter Creek Trail is a favorite winter route for hikers and dog walkers (dogs must be leashed). This is one of the few trails that can be accessed on foot from the center of Aspen. The route follows the beautiful boulder-filled Hunter Creek as it drops into Aspen from between Smuggler Mountain and Red Mountain out of Hunter Valley. This much-used trail is always packed out, so only boots are necessary; however, it would be wise to use cleats and/or poles, since traction on the steep upper half of the narrow trail can sometimes be a problem. After a heavy snow snowshoes could be used. This trail also provides access to the Hunter Valley Trail (see Route #17), a good extension for a longer hike.

Route

From the signed trailhead, follow the packed trail along a wooden fence as it drops down to Hunter Creek and then follows the creek through the trees. At .3 miles the trail crosses a bridge over the creek and then another bridge over an irrigation ditch. As the trail starts climbing, the way opens up in the scrub oak. Smuggler Mountain rises on the right and Red Mountain on the left as the trail heads up the drainage. Over another bridge, at one-half mile, the trail junctions with the Lani White Trail which heads right toward the Centennial Condominiums. Continue left on a steep uphill climb which leads to another bridge over the creek. The rest of the route climbs steeply along the left side of the creek, at times working its way around large boulders. At just under 1 mile you reach the Hunter Valley Trail crossing over the Benedict Bridge. This is a good turnaround point, or you can continue right across the bridge and up toward Hunter Valley.

Top: One of the bridges for the trail over Hunter Creek
Bottom right: The snow-covered, bouldered Hunter Creek

Hunter Valley

MAPS: TI #127, Aspen/Snowmass Outdoors

DISTANCE: 3–4 miles, or more; reservoir bridge loop is 4.2 miles

ELEVATION: 8,300–9,000 feet

ACCESS: In the winter the access to Hunter Valley is from the Hunter Creek Trail parking lot (different than the trailhead for Route #16). To get there, take Mill Street north from Main Street (by the Hotel Jerome). After crossing the bridge over the Roaring Fork, bear left onto Red Mountain Road and follow it steeply uphill to Hunter Creek Road (1.3 miles from Main Street). Go right for .3 miles, then left up a hill into the Hunter Creek Trail parking lot. Avoid the private driveways, watch for signs.

Comments

Summer and winter, Hunter Valley is one of the most popular trips from Aspen because of its beauty, accessibility, and peaceful setting. Hunter Valley has everything you would expect from an idyllic mountain valley: the picturesque Hunter Creek with snow-covered boulders, the meadowed valley floor, the surrounding mountain peaks, the prominent Thimble Rock at the end of the valley, wildlife, the abandoned hunters' cabins and much more. You can spend anywhere from 2 hours to all day on your tour in Hunter Valley. This is a good tour both on snowshoes and cross-country skis. Some of the options for side tours off the basic reservoir bridge loop include going up the backside of Smuggler Mountain, continuing to the end of Hunter Valley, and following the route to Van Horn Park/McNamara Hut.

Route

From the trailhead parking lot walk down to the road and go left through two large stone pillars. In about one-quarter mile, after a sharp turn in the road, the start of the trail will be on the right traversing along the side of the hill, with a sign saying "Hunter

Creek Trail". Put on your skis/snowshoes here. The trail traverses about 100 yards to the Benedict Bridge which crosses Hunter Creek. From the bridge the trail goes up fairly steeply for a while along the right side of Hunter Creek in the trees before leveling out somewhat. In less than a half mile, the route crosses a private road and continues through the trees.

Coming out of the trees at the National Forest boundary sign, you will see Hunter Valley opening up before you, with the creek to the left and mountains on all sides. A little farther ahead on the left, across the river, are the remains of old houses with tin roofs. Continuing straight ahead, in one-tenth mile you pass a sign to Smuggler Mountain indicating a trail to the right. This makes a good side trip off the basic loop, but involves a bit of climbing up the backside of Smuggler Mountain. Staying straight ahead on the reservoir bridge loop, you will soon draw even with the tin-roofed houses that lie on the other side of the creek, and see a side trail going down on the left to the 10th Mountain Bridge across Hunter Creek. This is the route to McNamara, Margy's, and other 10th Mountain huts. This is also access to the large meadows of Van Horn Park (2 miles up with a climb of almost 1,000 feet) which provide some good open telemark skiing or an extensive snowshoe tour.

For the basic loop, continue straight along the right side of Hunter Creek on the trail. In .75 mile you'll see the remains of a cabin across the river and will come to a small bridge ("reservoir bridge") over the river. If you turn right here, you can follow an old jeep trail than angles back toward Smuggler Mountain and loops back to the earlier trail up the backside of Smuggler Mountain. However, to stay on the basic loop, take a left over reservoir bridge. Immediately on the other side of the bridge you can diverge from the basic route again by going right and following a trail along the left side of the river for another mile or so. You will pass the remains of two cabins to the side of a large meadow and eventually will have to turn back in the trees as the valley narrows, but not before encountering one more abandoned cabin. The mass of rock that looms ahead at the end of the valley is 10,130-foot Thimble Rock.

Continuing on the basic loop at reservoir bridge, head back down the valley along the right side of Hunter Creek through the fields. In .75 miles, just past the abandoned cabins with the tin roofs, turn left to cross over the 10th Mountain Bridge, beyond which you go right to head back to the trailhead to complete the 4.2-mile reservoir bridge loop. You could also have continued straight past these cabins to hook up with the road that climbs up to the right to Van Horn Park and to the McNamara Hut. So many choices!

Top: *The "reservoir bridge" over Hunter Creek in Hunter Valley*
Bottom: *The snow-covered boulders of Hunter Creek in Hunter Valley*

Smuggler Mountain Road

MAP: Aspen/Snowmass Outdoors

DISTANCE: 1.5 miles round trip to the Platform; 12 miles round trip to Warren Lakes and the Benedict Huts

ELEVATION: 8,000–8,800 feet (Platform), 8,000–11,000 feet (Benedict Huts)

ACCESS: Go north on Mill Street from the Hotel Jerome in Aspen to the river. After crossing the bridge turn right on Gibson and go up a short steep hill. At the top bear left on South Ave., staying right on South Ave. (Park Circle) at the intersection with Spruce Street. In a quarter mile, just past the Centennial Condominiums, the Smuggler Mountain Road switchbacks up the side of the mountain on the left. Parking is available on Park Circle.

Comments

The accessibility of this road to Aspen, the steepness, and the fantastic views of Aspen along the way are all factors in making this route one of the most popular in Aspen for a good workout, or for walking the dog, both during the summer and winter. In the winter the preferred mode of travel is boots if you are just going to the Platform (the trail is always well packed), or snowshoes if you are continuing towards Warren Lakes and the Benedict Huts. The popular turnaround point is the "Platform", a viewpoint overlooking Aspen at the end of a steep steady climb. For those hardcore snowshoers or skiers looking for a long workout and an enjoyable excursion into the forest atop Smuggler Mountain, it is possible to continue all the way to Warren Lakes where the 10th Mountain Benedict Huts are located. If you do reach the Benedict Huts, remember they are reserved for private use by skiers. Also be aware that much of the upper route beyond the Platform may be unbroken trail. You must be in good shape and acclimated to make this long, steep trip.

Route

Start on the switchbacks, staying to the right of the Smuggler Mine at the beginning. Be aware of the private driveways during the first part of the route. Continue on the long steady climb up the side of Smuggler Mountain until you eventually round a curve and head into the woods on the right. The Platform, the usual destination, will be on your right up a short steep bank. Take the time to enjoy the views of Aspen and the Roaring Fork Valley.

To continue on, follow the road to the right as it slowly climbs along the side of Smuggler Mountain with more good views of Aspen. At the open area one-half mile above the Platform, stay right into the woods and up some steep switchbacks for a mile of steady climbing to a large microwave reflector on the right. At this point the climb gets even steeper, but after one-half mile or so, the route levels out for a pleasant walk through the woods for the last 2.5 miles to the Benedict Huts.

Snowshoers at the trail fork to the Benedict Huts

Sunnyside Trail

MAPS: Aspen/Snowmass Outdoors, TI #127

DISTANCE: 5 miles round trip to communications towers

ELEVATION: 7,860–9,350 feet

ACCESS: Go west on Highway 82 from Aspen to Cemetery Lane just over the Castle Creek bridge and go right on Cemetery Lane for 1.5 miles (one-third mile past the bridge over the Roaring Fork River) to a small parking area on the left. The trailhead is just across the road.

If on foot, take the Snowbunny Bus to Red Butte Drive and walk another .4 miles uphill on McLain Flats Road (continuation of Cemetery Lane) to the trailhead on the right.

Comments

The Sunnyside Trail ascends steeply up the southwest face of Red Mountain just outside Aspen and affords outstanding views of Aspen, the upper Roaring Fork Valley and the ski areas and mountains in the Aspen area. The usually-packed trail can generally be hiked in boots, but snowshoes may be necessary after a heavy snowfall. It is too narrow and steep for skis. The south-facing trail gets a lot of sun and can be muddy or even bare of snow during periods of low snow. The route up, with a few reprieves, is steep as it gains 1,500 feet in 2.5 miles. The goal is to reach the communication towers, but the top part may require you to posthole in deep snow in the trees at the top. Snowshoers can continue past the towers along the ridge if they have the time and energy. The spectacular views can be enjoyed all along the route on this out-and-back hike, so anywhere along the way can be used as a turnaround point. Stay on the trail to avoid private property along the way.

Route

From the trailhead the trail climbs through the scrub oak, sagebrush and bushes, then flattens out as it follows an irrigation ditch a mile up from the road. Across the valley Hayden Peak, Pyramid Peak, Mount Daly and Mount Sopris stand out prominently. After crossing the ditch, the trail heads uphill, taking long switchbacks up the steep hillside for over a mile until you reach the aspen trees. The snow gets deeper in the trees as you climb the last 100 feet in elevation to reach some communication towers at 9,350 feet elevation. This affords some good views and a good spot to turn around.

Top: Looking toward Highlands and Buttermilk from Sunnyside
Bottom left & right: On the Sunnyside Trail overlooking the Roaring Fork Valley

Maroon Creek Trail

MAPS: Aspen/Snowmass Outdoors, TI #128

DISTANCE: 3 miles roundtrip, or more if connecting with the Owl Creek Trail

ELEVATION: 7,790–7,980 feet

ACCESS: By car, drive one mile west of Aspen on Highway 82 (one-half mile beyond the roundabout) to the Aspen Cross-Country Center at the golf course on the right. Parking is plentiful. By bus, take the local valley bus to the Truscott Place stop. By foot, you can ski or snowshoe across the Marolt Bridge on the west end of Aspen, staying right through the Marolt Property and follow the signs to cross under Highway 82 and follow the trail to the Aspen Cross-Country Center.

Comments

Snowshoers looking for a scenic snowshoe route close to Aspen will really enjoy this trail along the river, especially after a fresh snow. The trail is easily accessible from the Aspen Cross-Country Center at the golf course, or from the Tiehack base area. This route along Maroon Creek lies below the hubbub above and is seldom used or found by the crowd. The route as described is an out-and-back to where the trail ends at a water gauging station, but it can also be used to access the Owl Creek Trail at Tiehack. Snowshoes can be rented at the Aspen Cross-Country Center.

Route

Starting at the Aspen Cross-Country Center go along Bernese Blvd. heading west for about 100 yards to the west end of the golf course and look for an old roadbed/trail that angles down to the left into the valley under the high span of the Maroon Creek Bridge. The trail may or may not have tracks on it, so don't miss it. Once on the trail you will be dropping down under the Maroon Creek Bridge and will cross the creek over a narrow, wooden bridge, the Bob Helm Bridge. Continue left of the other side of the creek on a route that overlooks the winter creek setting of

Maroon Creek. In half a mile the trail switchbacks up the valley wall and comes to an intersection with a trail going off to the right. That trail leads to the Maroon Creek Club tracks and to the Buttermilk Ski Area. Stay left on the Maroon Creek Trail as it continues on its traverse above the river. At one mile from the start, the trail crosses under the Tiehack Bridge and comes to a trail intersection. Stay straight—going to the right will take you up to the west end of the Tiehack Bridge, the Tiehack Base Area and the Owl Creek Trail. The signed Government Trail isn't usable at this point in the winter. Staying along Maroon Creek on a level route you soon come to a water gauging station and the end of the Maroon Creek Trail. This is your turnaround point and you can continue back to the Cross-Country Center for a 3-mile round trip, or go up to Tiehack on the way back and continue on the Owl Creek Trail from the Tiehack Base Area.

Top: *Looking down at Maroon Creek from the Maroon Trail*
Bottom Right: *The Bob Helm Bridge over Maroon Creek*

Maroon Creek Road

MAPS: Aspen/Snowmass Outdoors, TI #128, TI #127

DISTANCE: 6.2 miles one way to Maroon Lake

ELEVATION: 8,200–9,600 feet

ACCESS: Take Highway 82 west from Aspen one-half mile to the roundabout and exit onto Maroon Creek Road toward Aspen Highlands. Go 3.3 miles up the road to the end of the plowed section of the Maroon Creek Road at the T Lazy 7 Ranch and park.

Comments

Maroon Creek Road leads to Maroon Lake and three 14,000-foot mountains—Pyramid Peak, North Maroon Peak and South Maroon Peak (the Maroon Bells—the most photographed mountains in the country). Summer visitors are familiar with the drive to Maroon Lake, but most winter visitors don't realize the road is also available to cross-country skiers, snowshoers and hikers from its closure at the T Lazy 7 Ranch. This route is good for taking an all-day trip with a picnic stop, either at Maroon Lake beneath the Maroon Bells, or somewhere along Maroon Creek. Since the route is usually well-packed out by snowmobiles, snowshoes are not always necessary; skis, however, are the preferred mode of travel. Dogs on leash are allowed. Generally, traffic along this route is heavier on the weekends, so on Saturdays and Sundays expect to encounter some snowmobile traffic. The road is plenty wide, however, to accommodate skiers, snowshoers, hikers and snowmobilers.

The road follows the west side of Maroon Creek very gently uphill all the way to the lake. The valley has steep walls and is avalanche prone in many spots. Whenever the avalanche danger is high, however, the road is closed beyond the T Lazy 7 to any kind of traffic.

Route

As you head up the snow-packed road, one of the most prominent peaks in the area, the rugged 14,018-foot Pyramid Peak, looms directly ahead of you. Maroon Creek follows the road on the left. You also may see some signs of avalanches that have come down from the steep valley walls—trees get flattened and wide paths are cleared by the tumbling snow. From time to time some of these avalanches may even come across the road, forcing the route to close. At 1.5 miles you pass the Welcome Station and Silver Bar Campground. The Silver Queen Campground is at 2.8 miles. The road bearing down to the left at 3.1 miles, at the East Maroon Wilderness Portal, can be taken as a side trip to cross Maroon Creek and follow the trail on the other side of the creek. East Maroon Portal marks the halfway point to Maroon Lake. At 4.3 miles, where Maroon Creek Road bends to the right, Pyramid Peak dominates the middle of the main valley, the side valley going off to the left is East Maroon Valley, and you see the Maroon Bells ahead to the right for the first time. This sight alone is worth the trip.

For the next couple of miles the Maroon Bells stand out in all their glory ahead of you, giving you many photo opportunities. At 6 miles you reach the parking areas. Follow the packed road to its end at 6.2 miles by the summer bunkers and a small warming shack where the T Lazy 7 usually has hot drinks available for skiers and snowmobilers. You have a magnificent view of the Maroon Bells as you look across Maroon Lake with the end of valley sloping up beyond the lake. Around the basin formed by the lake are some steep slopes, often with signs of slides. The return trip down is a very gradual downhill all the way, making the return a lot easier than the trip up, especially for skiers.

LEFT: *Pyramid Peak looms over Maroon Creek Road*
RIGHT: *Nearing the Bells on Maroon Creek Road*

Midnight Mine Road

MAPS: Aspen/Snowmass Outdoors, TI #127

DISTANCE: 4.5 miles one way to the Sundeck (from end-of-road parking)

ELEVATION: 8,590–11,212 feet

ACCESS: Take Highway 82 west from Aspen one-half mile to the roundabout and exit onto Castle Creek Road toward the hospital and Ashcroft. Go 2.7 miles up Castle Creek Road to the Midnight Mine Road angling down to the left. Follow the Midnight Mine Road .8 miles to designated parking at the end of the plowed road.

Comments

For skiers and snowshoers the Midnight Mine Road provides a scenic, mostly wooded route up the backside of Aspen Mountain to the Sundeck and the top of Richmond Ridge. The road passes several old mines, and higher up offers spectacular views up the Castle Creek Valley. This route is less steep and more scenic than the uphill route going up the front side of Aspen Mountain (see Route #1) and can be done any time of the day. This route can also be used by skiers to skin up to Little Annie Basin for some turns. Be aware of the private property along the road, and stay on the main road to the top. You may encounter some snowmobile traffic, especially on the weekends.

Remnants of the historic Midnight Mine

Route

Put on your snowshoes or skis with skins and follow the road as it begins its climb along the left side of Queen's Gulch. At 1.1 miles up the road you'll pass a road angling up to the right to Horseshoe Lode. At 1.6 miles you'll pass the remains of the Midnight Mine and will climb steeply over the tailings as you cross over Queens Gulch for some long switchbacks through the trees. At 3.2 miles (10,680 feet), as you have spectacular views to the right of Highlands Bowl, Five Fingers, Hayden Peak and its ridge, you come to a road fork with Little Annie Basin lying ahead. Follow the left fork to gently climb the last 1.3 miles to the Sundeck, which is visible in the distance atop Aspen Mountain as soon as you break into the open. The road going right at this fork is the Little Annie Road (see Route #23). From the Sundeck, retrace your route back to the car.

Approaching the Sundeck on the Midnight Mine Road

Little Annie Road

MAPS: Aspen/Snowmass Outdoors, TI #127

DISTANCE: 4.5 miles one-way to the Sundeck
(from Castle Creek Road)

ELEVATION: 9,000–11,212 feet

ACCESS: Take Highway 82 west from Aspen one-half mile to the roundabout and exit onto Castle Creek Road toward the hospital and Ashcroft. Go 6.8 miles up Castle Creek Road to the Little Annie Road on the left. A pull-out for parking is on the right, or there is a designated parking area for several cars about 200 yards up the Little Annie Road. It is not advisable to drive any further up the road. (See Route #22 for access directions for a car drop on Midnight Mine Road if you are doing a loop.)

Comments

The Little Annie Road is a shorter ascent up the back of Aspen Mountain to the Sundeck on skis or snowshoes than the Midnight Mine Road, and offers even better views of the valley and surrounding peaks. Hayden Peak, Highland Peak, Five Fingers, Highlands Bowl and the ridges flanking the valleys provide a picturesque winter landscape. Since most of the route is open and south-facing, snow conditions may deteriorate faster in the spring than on Midnight Mine Road, so plan your trip accordingly. The first 1.5 miles of the road is plowed, so you will have to hike this portion from your car carrying your skis or snowshoes. This route is best done during the week, since on weekends Little Annie Road is heavily used by snowmobiles. This route can also be combined with a trip down Midnight Mine Road to offer a little more variety and a great 8–10 mile loop from Castle Creek Road. For this option you will need a car drop.

Route

The first section of road climbs past a few homes and is plowed for the first 1.5 miles to 9,640 feet, where it cuts back into Hurricane Gulch. Put on your snowshoes or skis with skins and start up the fairly steep climb first through the open, then trees to where the road finally breaks out into Little Annie Basin, a large, open park. The road switchbacks up through the basin until it meets Midnight Mine Road at 3.2 miles (10,715 feet). Bearing right here will take you past a second junction for the Midnight Mine Road by a cabin from where you can see the Sundeck ahead on top of Aspen Mountain in the distance. Continuing ahead toward the Sundeck you soon enter the trees and climb gently the last mile to the Sundeck, from where you can backtrack to your car, or return down Midnight Mine Road to where you dropped a second car. It is 3.2 miles down Midnight Mine Road from the junction with Little Annie Road. Whatever route you choose, it will be an adventure you'll always remember.

Highlands Ridge seen from Little Annie Road

Richmond Ridge

MAPS: Aspen/Snowmass Outdoors, TI #127

DISTANCE: Up to 10 miles round trip to be safe; Richmond Ridge can be skied or snowshoed much farther, but the area becomes more difficult and avalanche prone

ELEVATION: 11,000–11,570 feet

ACCESS: Richmond Ridge is reached by taking the Silver Queen Gondola (for a fee) to the top of Aspen Mountain and then going off the back (south) side and following the tracks made by snowcats and snowmobiles. For the very energetic and fit, Midnight Mine Road (Route #22), Little Annie Road (Route #23), or the early morning uphill route up the front of Aspen Mountain (Route #1) can all be used to reach Richmond Ridge.

Comments

Richmond Ridge extends from the top of Aspen Mountain to the south, forming the eastern ridge of the Castle Creek Valley. From this vantage point skiers and snowshoers have a great view of Hayden Peak, the Maroon Bells, Pyramid Peak, Highlands Bowl, Independence Pass, and many of the surrounding mountains in the Maroon Bells–Snowmass Wilderness. Most skiers or snowshoers use Richmond Ridge as a day tour, riding the Silver Queen Gondola up Aspen Mountain to get to the start of the tour and doing an out-and-back on the ridge any distance they want. The route follows Richmond Ridge Road which goes all the way to Taylor Pass, a distance of about 11 miles. The route is also used by backcountry skiers to get to the Barnard Hut in the Braun Hut System.

Since the whole route is above 11,000 feet, cold and windy weather can make this trip miserable, and the visibility can also be quite bad at times. In good weather, however, Richmond Ridge gives the best overall views of the mountains of any of the routes in this part of the state. The snow also holds up well late into the season because of the high elevation. The road is packed by snowcats and snowmobiles for the beginning part of the route. For your return, be sure to check the time for the last gondola ride back down Aspen Mountain (usually around 4:00 p.m.).

Route

The route follows the ridge, so keeping this in mind it's hard to get lost. The first part is a gradual uphill. Some of the route is in the open with scattered trees, while other parts go through the trees. To the right you will be looking across the Castle Creek and Maroon Creek valleys. Farther off to the west Mount Sopris dominates the skyline. To the south you will be looking toward Crested Butte, and to the left up the Roaring Fork Valley toward Independence Pass, the Sawatch Range, and the Collegiate Peaks. Behind you to the north is Aspen, the Williams Range, Hunter Valley, Red and Smuggler mountains. This is all fantastic scenery, to say the least.

Follow the packed road as it stays near the ridge, going around the left side of a steep knob at about one-half mile. This will keep you on the left (east) side of Richmond Ridge with views up the valley toward Independence Pass. At .9 miles you come to a short, very steep uphill as you continue on top of the ridge. Off to the right the Maroon Bells and Pyramid Peak appear beyond the next ridge. The ridge continues with gradual ups and downs, always with good views in every direction.

Hayden Peak, up ahead to the right on the other side of the Castle Creek Valley, is one that many backcountry skiers climb in the spring to ski. This was to be the original ski area in Aspen. The first valley on the right is Castle Creek; the other side of the wooded ridge is Maroon Creek Valley.

At 1.7 miles (11,400 feet), after descending a hill, the snowcat-packed road (used for powder tours) will angle down to the left, but stay right to ascend to the top of the ridge and more spectacular views. At 2 miles you will reach a high point of 11,570 feet. As you keep following the ridge back, you will encounter a mixture of trees, open spots, and little knolls. Eventually, after a couple more miles you will reach some large, flat meadows. From here the trail drops down for a while into McFarlane Gulch; generally this is a good place to turn around. If you follow the trail any farther (more difficult and avalanche prone) watch for the diamonds on the trees marking the trail.

West Buttermilk Ridge

MAPS: TI #128, USGS quad Highland Peak

DISTANCE: 2.2 miles one way to the Sugar Bowl from the bottom of West Buttermilk, 1 mile one way from the top of the West Buttermilk ski lift to the bowl, 4.5 miles round trip doing a loop from West Buttermilk parking up the ski slopes, along the ridge and down through the Sugar Bowl and out on the Government Trail back to West Buttermilk

ELEVATION: 8,820 (parking lot)/9,900(top of West Buttermilk lift)–10,120 feet (high point on ridge before the bowls)

ACCESS: Take Highway 82 and turn south at the stoplight (Owl Creek Road), the main entrance to the Buttermilk Ski Area west of Aspen. Just past the ski area parking, turn left onto West Buttermilk Road. Follow the road going uphill from that point for 3 miles, to its end, and park in the public parking area for West Buttermilk (8,820 feet) for the hike up West Buttermilk. You can also take the high-speed chairlift from Main Buttermilk to the top and hike a little further up to the top of West Buttermilk.

Comments

The ridge from the top of the West Buttermilk ski lift heads high above Willow Creek along the edge of the Maroon Bells–Snowmass Wilderness toward Burnt Mountain and the Snowmass Ski Area. To the east and south are tremendous vistas of the Maroon Creek Valley, Aspen Highlands, and the Willow Creek Valley. Burnt Mountain lies directly ahead to the west. Extra clothing is recommended on this trip as weather can change quickly and you will be above 10,000 feet. Also, be aware that the route along the ridge may be untracked and the snow could be quite deep. For skiers skins are recommended for the steady climb along the ridge.

For the normal tour, use this route as an out-and-back from the bottom of West Buttermilk or from the top of the West Buttermilk ski lift. The more adventurous telemark or alpine touring skiers can follow the ridge to the Sugar Bowl on the right and ski down to the Government Trail above Whites Lake, and then follow the trail back to West Buttermilk. The even more adventurous and experienced skier or snowshoer can follow the ridge all the way to Burnt Mountain and the Elk Camp section of the Snowmass Ski Area. However, this trip requires backcountry experience and knowledge of avalanche conditions.

Route

From the top of the West Buttermilk chairlift go to the backcountry gate behind the warming hut to start. Stay on the top of the ridge as it begins a steady climb above Willow Creek. One-third mile from the lift enjoy the overlook with its views to Aspen Highlands, up Maroon Creek Valley and into Willow Creek Valley on the right. At this point the ridge turns to the right and leads high above Willow Creek. From here on the trail is mostly narrow and in the trees. Avoid dropping off to the side of the ridge if at all possible.

The route levels off somewhat as it leads to the clearings on the right (the Sugar Bowl) and a drop in elevation. This is a good place to turn around if you've had enough, or if you're on skis take your skins off and ski down through the clearings and aspens to the Government Trail for the return loop to the West Buttermilk Ski Area. Have a good map and altimeter to pick up the trail at about 9,300 feet elevation.

For experienced backcountry skiers you can continue toward Burnt Mountain which you see ahead on the right. Follow the ridge to where you can safely traverse and climb around the front side of Burnt Mountain and drop to the top of the Elk Camp area. You have to climb some fairly steep slopes to get up around Burnt Mountain, so be very aware of avalanche conditions and travel with other skiers/snowshoers. Use your map and compass; an altimeter would be very useful here also. From Snowmass you can take the skier shuttle bus back to Buttermilk (only if you get there soon enough—check the schedules ahead of time).

Government Trail

MAPS: Aspen/Snowmass Outdoors, TI #128

DISTANCE: 8.8 miles roundtrip from West Buttermilk to the Two Creeks chair lift

ELEVATION: 8,800–9,440 feet

ACCESS: Take Highway 82 and turn south at the stoplight (Owl Creek Road), the main entrance to the Buttermilk Ski Area west of Aspen. Just past the ski area parking, turn left onto West Buttermilk Road. Follow the road going uphill from that point for 3 miles, to its end, and park in the public parking area for West Buttermilk (8,820 feet).

The trail can also be accessed from the Two Creeks Ski Area: take the Two Creeks lift up and ski or snowshoe down to lift tower #24 where you will see the trail going off to the right (not well marked).

Comments

The Government Trail, a peaceful, infrequently traveled, wooded trail between West Buttermilk and the Two Creeks Ski Area in Snowmass, provides skiers and snowshoers with a backcountry experience close to home. The trail passes through magnificent stands of aspen and evergreens, making it one of the most beautiful wooded cross-country trails around. Yet, the Government Trail has not been "discovered" by the many cross-country skiers in the area. The trail is marked, although not well, by some blue diamonds, trail markings on the trees, and a couple of signs. On the Snowmass end, occasional orange diamonds (for snowmobile trails) mark part of the route. The trail is not used much except by animals and a few skiers and snowshoers, so it may not be packed. Be prepared for deep snow and occasional route-finding challenges. A map can be very helpful.

The trail is best done as an out-and-back from West Buttermilk since access to the trail in Snowmass Village can only be done by climbing the eastern slopes at Two Creeks. On the way back to

West Buttermilk, a higher route can be followed for the last mile (see description).

Route

(From West Buttermilk). Traverse (angling up) across the West Buttermilk slope under the chair lift to the right hand side. Just up the slope on the right at the bottom of the Lower Larkspur ski run is a trail going into the woods (8,890 feet) with a sign warning that you're entering the backcountry. Just beyond the sign is a gate that marks the beginning of the route, which is a spur access for the Government Trail. (The actual Government Trail comes into West Buttermilk higher up the slope where it can be accessed from the Red's Rover ski run, but the lower access is more commonly used.) The route follows a roadcut and steadily contours uphill through the tall stands of aspen, following a gully, and then crossing over the gully and continuing up until it reaches the ridge where it levels off somewhat. As the trail rounds a corner with views out over the valley, at .75 miles (9,075 feet), a side trail on the left going straight uphill with a sign to the Government Trail will appear. Take the steep uphill ascent (following the occasional blue diamond marker) through the aspen.

At 1.0 miles (9,250 feet), you will come to an intersection with a trail going left. This is where the Government Trail comes in from West Buttermilk. Stay right to continue toward Snowmass, but remember this intersection for the preferred return route to West Buttermilk. The trail continues above White's Lake; at 1.45 miles (9,375 feet), stay straight as a trail/road goes down to the right.

The Government Trail continues through the aspen as it levels off a little, contouring through the trees into a beautiful, peaceful, pine forest with an occasional spruce. At 2.4 miles (9,360 feet), you pass through a fence line in the tall evergreens. From there an easy descent follows as the trail gradually returns to more aspen. At the far end of an open meadow, at 3.25 miles (9,060 feet), there will be a sign indicating the intersection with the Anaerobic Nightmare Trail. Follow the Government Trail as it bears left up the slope. In another half mile (3.7 miles, 9,115 feet) the trail reaches the Two Creek Ski Area boundary, a possible turnaround point. However, more great terrain and spectacular scenery lies ahead.

Traverse across the Long Shot ski run and continue back into the trees following the blue/orange diamonds. From this point on, there are some ups and downs as the trail meanders through a couple of gullies. After crossing the East Brush Creek gully (4.1 miles, 9,170 feet), the trail ascends a short way through the aspen to the ski slopes and the Two Creeks chair lift (4.4 miles, 9,215 feet). This makes a good destination and turnaround point, as the trail is not marked beyond this point as it crosses the busy ski slopes. If you ski down the ski slopes, you could catch a bus from Two Creeks or Snowmass back to Aspen or Buttermilk, but there is no bus service up the West Buttermilk Road.

On your return trip to West Buttermilk on the Government Trail, bear right at the intersection for the Government Trail that you noted on the way one mile into the ski/snowshoe (look for a blue diamond). Following the trail back to Buttermilk will take you on a high, narrow contour along a steep slope through the aspen for one-half mile to the Red's Rover ski Run at West Buttermilk. Follow Red's Rover down under the chair lift to the right to get back to the parking lot.

Trail intersection for the high and low return routes to West Buttermilk

Owl Creek Trail

MAP: Aspen/Snowmass Council Nordic map

DISTANCE: Aspen XC Center to Tiehack via Moore Trail (1.1 miles),
Tiehack to West Buttermilk Road (1.5 miles), West
Buttermilk Road to Sinclair Divide (3.3 miles), Sinclair
Divide to Two Creeks slopes (.7 miles), Two Creeks
slopes (east end) to Snowmass Cross-Country Center
(2 miles)

ELEVATION: Aspen Cross-Country Center 7,880'; Tiehack Base Area
8,060'; West Buttermilk Road 8,450'; Sinclair Divide
8,390'; Two Creeks slopes—east end 8,160'; Snowmass
Cross-Country Center 7,950'

Comments

This popular trail connects Aspen and Snowmass Village, hugging
the south side of the Roaring Fork and Owl Creek valleys. The Owl
Creek Trail, a part of the Aspen/Snowmass Nordic Trail System, is
packed and tracked by pisten-bully snowcats and is easy to follow
as it crosses through occasional groves of aspen and traverses
wide open meadows. Most skiers and snowshoers use this trail as
a casual tour or workout; only light touring gear or skating skis
are needed. The trail can be accessed from a number of points
on the Aspen end, but only from the Snowmass Cross-Country
Center or Two Creeks on the Snowmass end.

The easiest and most popular stretch of trail runs from the West
Buttermilk Road to Sinclair Divide and then down to the Snowmass
Cross-Country Trail System. The most common trip is taking
the trail from West Buttermilk to Sinclair Divide and back—6.5
miles roundtrip. For the energetic skier or snowshoer, the trail
can be taken all the way from the Aspen Cross-Country Center
to the Snowmass Cross-Country Center or vice versa—8.6 miles
one way—and then taking the bus back or doubling back. The
trail can also be taken on an out-and-back trip any distance from
the Snowmass Cross-Country Center, a hilly trip at best and less
interesting than the trip from West Buttermilk. For the advanced

skier however, adding on the 3-mile hilly Terminator Loop makes for a good scenic workout from the Snowmass Cross-Country Center. No good access exists for the Owl Creek Trail between the Snowmass Cross-Country Center and West Buttermilk, except from the Two Creeks Base Area.

---------------- **TO START FROM THE ASPEN GOLF COURSE** ----------------

DISTANCE: To West Buttermilk Road 2.6 miles roundtrip; to Sinclair Divide 9.2 miles roundtrip; to Snowmass Cross-Country Center 8.6 miles one way

ACCESS: From the Aspen Cross-Country Center parking lot at the Aspen Golf Course one mile west of Aspen, cross under Highway 82 through the underpass (carrying your equipment) and walk along Highway 82 about 50 yards toward Aspen to the trailhead for the Moore Trail on the right. (From Aspen or the Aspen Recreation Center follow the Nordic tracks to the Tiehack Nordic Bridge).

Aspen Golf Course Route

Follow the groomed and tracked Moore Trail one mile to the Tiehack Nordic Bridge, staying right at any intersections. Snowshoers should stay along the edge of the packed trail. Go across on the Tiehack Nordic Bridge over Maroon Creek to the Tiehack Ski Area on the other side.

From the Tiehack Base Area the trail heads to the right of the small building and uphill along the right side of the slope; it is marked by green disks indicating "Owl Creek Trail". A long steady climb gets you to Main Buttermilk at .8 miles from Tiehack where you will be traversing across the slope, and to the snowboard park. Watch carefully (easy to miss) for a way to cut through the park and pick up the Owl Creek Trail angling back uphill to the right. The trail exits the ski area and continues uphill through the trees to a high point from where it descends through the aspen a short distance to West Buttermilk Road at 1.5 miles from Tiehack. Go left up the road for about 50 yards to pick up the continuation of the trail (well-signed) on the other side at the small trailhead parking area.

DISTANCE: To Sinclair Divide 6.6 miles roundtrip; to Two Creeks slopes 8 miles roundtrip; to Snowmass Cross-Country Center 12 miles roundtrip

ACCESS: Turn off Highway 82 at the entrance to the Buttermilk Ski Area west of Aspen and go to West Buttermilk Road on the left, just past the Buttermilk Ski Area parking. Turn onto West Buttermilk Road and drive up 1.7 miles to a small parking area on the right by the Owl Creek Trailhead signs.

West Buttermilk Road Route

From West Buttermilk Road the wide packed trail descends on a somewhat steep section through some trees. You will have to cross a driveway, the first of about 6 road crossings which may or may not require you to take off your skis. After some more woods the trail emerges into the large open fields where you have good views of the surrounding Owl Creek Valley. At this point the route is mostly flat, with some long gradual climbs and descents.

At 3.3 miles the route comes to a private road crossing at a high point in the trees—Sinclair Divide. Many skiers turn around here. Beyond the divide is a short, very steep downhill curving around to the right—the beginning of some gradual downhills which lead to the Two Creeks Ski Area slopes. The Terminator, a 3-mile expert loop goes off to the left of the Owl Creek Trail just below Sinclair Divide. Beyond the Terminator intersection continue to follow the green Owl Creek Trail markers. At 3.9 miles the trail enters the Two Creeks Ski Area, goes uphill to the right of a poma lift, turns left above the lift onto a gradual uphill up a ski slope. Soon a sharp uphill turn takes you under the ski lift and then down and up another ski slope until you clear the ski area for the final downhill to Owl Creek Road and the Snowmass Golf Course. The route may also be marked by orange Nordic trail markers at times. At 5.1 miles the route crosses Owl Creek Road and gets onto the Snowmass Cross-Country track system on the golf course. Follow the well-marked Owl Creek Trail downhill (mostly) through the golf course to the Cross-Country Center at the lower end of the golf course, crossing the Snowmass Club Road at 5.6 miles on the way to the Center.

MAIN ACCESS: Snowmass Cross-Country Center—By car from Aspen or Snowmass, take Brush Creek Road toward Snowmass Village, continue through the roundabout and in 200 yards look for a left turn across from the Rodeo Parking Lot to the Snowmass Golf Course Clubhouse where the Cross-Country Center is located. By bus take any Snowmass Village bus to the Rodeo Lot, cross the street and walk a couple of hundred yards up Clubhouse Drive to the Cross-Country Center.

SECONDARY: From Two Creeks Base Area (you can pay
ACCESS   park at Two Creeks or take a village bus to Two Creeks)—Go up the slope from the base area to the Owl Creek Trail marked by the green markers and head toward Aspen (see route description below).

The Owl Creek Valley and Mt. Daly

Route

Starting from the Snowmass Cross-Country Center follow the green Owl Creek Trail markers up the hill on the golf course trails to a road crossing at .4 miles, and then the road crossing at the Owl Creek Road at .9 miles. Continue following the packed marked trail uphill to a left that takes you across the Two Creeks ski slopes. At 2 miles the trail exits the ski area at the base of a poma lift. From here the Oregon Trail continues up to a short steep uphill in the trees to Sinclair Divide, 2.7 miles from the cross-country center.

For the next 3.3 miles, follow the wide packed tracks of the Owl Creek Trail through the open, scenic Owl Creek Valley to a final climb to West Buttermilk Road.

On the other side of the road, you will climb through the trees a little farther to the high point of the trail. A short downhill through the trees takes you to the Buttermilk Ski Area where you follow the green disks left on a traverse across the ski slope and then onto the wide catwalk (Oregon Trail) to Tiehack and the Tiehack Base Area.

At Tiehack go straight across the road to cross the Tiehack Nordic Bridge. On the other side take a left onto the Moore tracks and head on a gradual descent on the groomed tracks (stay left at all intersections for the last mile to Highway 82). Take off your equipment, go left for 50 yards along the highway to an underpass (just past the stoplight) which takes you to the parking lot at the Aspen Cross-Country Center. There is also a bus stop here on Highway 82 for travel up or downvalley.

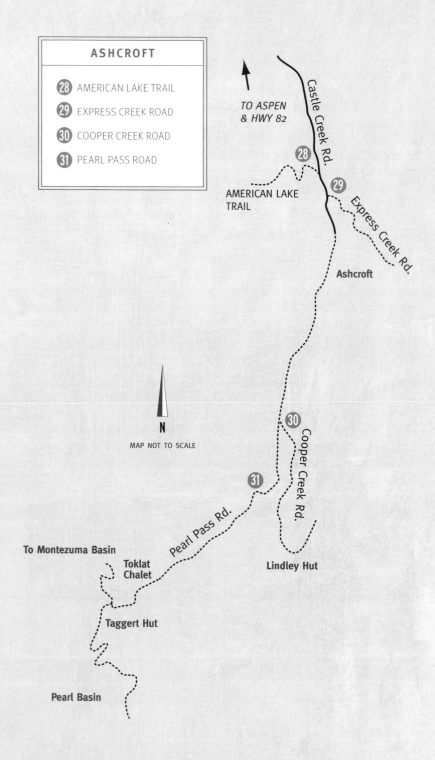

Castle Creek Road not only provides access to the packed trails at Ashcroft Ski Touring, but also to other nearby cross-country ski and snowshoe opportunities in the scenic historic Ashcroft area. Three snow-covered roads—Express Creek, Cooper Creek and Pearl Pass roads—lead up into the avalanche-prone mountains near Ashcroft. These routes require backcountry knowledge and experience for winter users. Also, the easily accessible American Lake Trail gives snowshoers and hikers a good workout as it ventures through the woods towards the high country. Before using any of these routes be sure to check with the Colorado Avalanche Information Center and/or Ashcroft Ski Touring for the latest avalanche conditions in the mountains at the upper end of the Castle Creek Valley.

American Lake Trail

MAPS: Aspen/Snowmass Outdoors, TI #127

DISTANCE: 2–4 steep miles roundtrip

ELEVATION: 9,400–10,600+

ACCESS: Take Highway 82 west from Aspen one-half mile to the roundabout and exit onto Castle Creek Road toward the hospital and Ashcroft. Go 10 miles up the road to parking on the right for the American Lake Trailhead.

Comments

The trail to American Lake is a popular summer hike, but can also be used in the winter by snowshoers or hikers for a good pleasant workout up through the aspen trees. The first mile or so of the trail is generally packed out by hikers/snowshoers. However, the narrowness and steepness of the trail makes it impractical for cross-country skiing. Since the route is heavily wooded, views are minimal. It is not practical or safe to take the trail all the way to American Lake, but it can be followed for up to 2 miles when avalanche danger is not high.

Route

Follow the trail out of the back of the parking lot past the trailhead sign and then across a relatively flat section before the steep climb begins through the aspen. The trail continues on a series of long switchbacks to the right of a small drainage. After about 1.5 miles the trail levels off somewhat at 10,600 feet and opens up. Be aware of the potential avalanche slopes up above on the right. Turn around at any point up here and retrace your route back.

Express Creek Road

MAPS: Aspen/Snowmass Outdoors, TI #127

DISTANCE: 4.6 miles roundtrip to the Markley Hut

ELEVATION: 9,440–10,700+

ACCESS: Take Highway 82 west from Aspen one-half mile to the roundabout and exit onto Castle Creek Road toward the hospital and Ashcroft. Go 11 miles up the road to parking on the left for Ashcroft.

Comments

Express Creek Road (Taylor Pass Road) climbs steeply from Ashcroft up the lovely Express Creek Valley along the western side of Ashcroft Mountain to 11,928-foot Taylor Pass and Richmond Ridge, the ridge which goes south from the top of Aspen Mountain. The road is used by backcountry skiers to access the Markley Hut, the Goodwin Greene Hut and the Barnard Hut— huts in the Alfred A. Braun Hut System. Express Creek Road crosses many avalanche paths and is best to explore during periods of low avalanche activity. The views from the road are memorable: the ghost town of Ashcroft, 14,265-foot Capitol Peak and other nearby summits, the high country above Express Creek Valley, etc. The steady uphill grade makes this both a good workout and a scenic trip for snowshoers and skiers wishing to get a taste of this high backcountry area. A logical turnaround point is the Markley Hut, but during periods of low avalanche activity, taking the road past the Markley Hut turnoff toward Richmond Ridge is a good way to see more epic high country in the winter. It is important not to travel this road during unsafe avalanche conditions. Check with the Colorado Avalanche Information Center for the latest conditions.

Route

From the parking area follow the packed track going across the open area northeast toward the snowpacked Express Creek Road and a bridge crossing the creek. Follow the road over the bridge as it begins its southeasterly climb along Ashcroft Mountain on the other side of Express Creek. As the road climbs through the trees the ghost town of Ashcroft is visible in the valley below. At one mile the road traverses across the first two avalanche paths. The next large avalanche path is less than one-half mile ahead. At just under 2 miles, after a climb of almost 1,000 feet from the valley floor, a trail forks down to the right with a sign for the Markley Hut. Following this route toward the hut through the trees avoids avalanche paths that lie up the road and makes for a good 5-mile tour. The Markley Hut (10,520 feet) is less than half a mile up the trail.

For those wishing to explore further under safe conditions, the road can be followed up across the more extreme avalanche paths from the Markley Hut turnoff intersection, or you can climb steeply up from the hut through the trees to intersect the road again. Either way, follow the road back to Ashcroft for the return trip.

TOP LEFT: *The Markley Hut*
BOTTOM LEFT: *Looking down at the ghost town of Ashcroft from Express Creek Road*
RIGHT: *An avalanche path above Express Creek Road*

ASHCROFT

30 Cooper Creek Road

MAP: TI #127

DISTANCE: 8 miles roundtrip (to Lindley Hut)

ELEVATION: 9,500–10,570 feet

ACCESS: Take Highway 82 west from Aspen one-half mile to the roundabout and exit onto Castle Creek Road toward the hospital and Ashcroft. Go 11 miles up the road to parking on the left for Ashcroft.

Comments

Cooper Creek Road was built to access an iron mine quarry south of Ashcroft at 12,000 feet near Taylor Peak. Although the mine never became productive, the road now serves as winter access to the Lindley Hut, one of the huts in the Alfred Braun Hut System. The road usually is tracked by users of the hut, making it a good day trip for cross-country skiers and snowshoers, who can also continue beyond the hut up the road. The high country above Cooper Creek, a tributary of Castle Creek, is some of the most spectacular in the Aspen area. The Elk Range, and especially 14,265-foot Castle Peak, stand out prominently across the valley from the road. Star Peak, at 13,521 feet, rises above Lindley Hut to the south.

The route from Ashcroft to the Lindley Hut and beyond can be very avalanche prone and should not be attempted during periods of high avalanche danger. Before attempting the trip, check both with the Colorado Avalanche Information Center and Ashcroft Ski Touring for the latest avalanche conditions.

Route

From the end of the plowed road in Ashcroft, go straight up the packed road (south) toward the end of the Castle Creek Valley. The road gradually heads uphill, passing the Pine Creek Cookhouse at 1.25 miles. From here the road continues on the valley floor, and at just under 2 miles comes to a junction with the old mine road going off to left (sign indicates Cooper Creek to the left, Pearl Pass and Montezuma Basin to the right). Head left up the road toward the Cooper Creek basin. In 300 yards the road crosses a bridge over Castle Creek, bears right and soon starts heading up to the left to get above the valley floor. The road climbs steadily above the Cooper Creek drainage with ever more spectacular views of Castle Peak and the Ridge of Gendarmes off to the west, and Star Peak to the south, looming above the Lindley Hut. At 3.9 miles, at a sharp bend in the road, a sign points down to the right for a short drop to the hut. The road continues to rise up to the left. This is a good place to turn around, or continue up the road if time and weather permit.

Top: Caution required on Cooper Creek Road
Bottom left: Heading toward the Elk Mountain Ridge
Bottom Right: Looking across Cooper Creek from the Lindley Hut

Pearl Pass Road

MAPS: TI #127, TI #131

DISTANCE: 6 miles one way into Pearl Basin, 5–12 miles roundtrip

ELEVATION: 9,500–12,000 feet

ACCESS: Take Highway 82 west from Aspen one-half mile to the roundabout and exit onto Castle Creek Road toward the hospital and Ashcroft. Go 11 miles up the road to parking on the left for Ashcroft.

Comments

This route follows Castle Creek Road and Pearl Pass Road from Ashcroft, past the Kellogg Cabin, along Castle Creek, past the Toklat Chalet (formerly The Mace Hut), past Tagert and Green Wilson huts, below 14,265-foot Castle Peak and into Pearl Basin. This is the perfect day trip for experienced skiers and snowshoers to enjoy some beautiful winter scenery in the backcountry, and for skiers to do a few turns in Pearl Basin. Only experienced backcountry skiers should venture past the Tagert and Green Wilson huts. The route is not groomed, so a trip up Pearl Pass Road may involve trail-breaking. A number of avalanche paths cross this route, both at the upper end of Castle Creek Valley and along Pearl Pass Road, so anyone taking this route should check with the Colorado Avalanche Information Center and with Ashcroft Ski Touring for the latest on avalanche danger. The first 2.5 miles on Castle Creek Road is very flat and perfect for beginner skiers or for snowshoers who wish to enjoy the beauty of the Castle Creek Valley.

Route

From the end of the plowed road in Ashcroft, go straight up the packed road (south) toward the end of the Castle Creek Valley. The road gradually heads uphill, passing the Pine Creek Cookhouse at 1.25 miles. From here the road continues on the valley floor and at just under 2 miles comes to a junction with the old mine road going off to left (sign indicates Cooper Creek to the left, Pearl Pass and Montezuma Basin to the right). Go right and follow this trail (Road 102) through the trees on the right side of the valley until it emerges into an avalanche slide path area. Stay right on the main road heading up the valley. Just after the road enters the trees, you come to a sign signifying the end of Ashcroft Ski Touring; on the right is the road to Kellogg Cabin. You are now about 2.5 miles from your start in Ashcroft.

To continue, go straight ahead on Pearl Pass Road, which heads uphill from this point along the right side of Castle Creek. The creek on the left cuts into rocks and forms a bit of a gorge. In about two-thirds of a mile from the Kellogg Cabin turnoff you cross over Castle Creek on a bridge. You will be continuing on the other side of the creek for the rest of way, climbing steadily through trees and some open areas. High mountain ridges marked with avalanche chutes rise up on each side. The uphill is steady, winding in some spots, but the trail is plenty wide. Finally, in a section of trees where the trail levels off a little, the Toklat Chalet (private property) will be somewhat hidden on the right. (This is almost 2 miles beyond the bridge, and a good 5 miles from the start.)

Junction with Old Mine Road

It takes most people 2.5 to 6 hours to get here, with the average being 3.5 hours. The elevation of the Toklat Chalet is 10,850 feet. The climb up past the Toklat Chalet to the Tagert Hut is less than a mile, a fairly steep uphill with switchbacks through rocky and narrow sections with some trees. Stay left at the fork with the road to Montezuma Basin. The Green Wilson Hut is a couple of hundred feet beyond the Tagert Hut. Pearl Basin starts opening up above you as you pass the huts. (Note that the Tagert and Green Wilson huts are part of the Braun Hut System and can be stayed in only through advance reservations.) This is a good turnaround point.

Advanced experienced skiers with time can continue to climb over a few ridges and knolls to emerge into the open basin. Stay on the left side of the basin as you work your way up. There are plenty of nice medium pitches to make turns coming down along this route. Pearl Basin is a beautiful alluring area surrounded by mountains, but is also very dangerous when avalanche danger is high. It is always best to go into Pearl Basin in a group, and to stay away from the steeper slopes. Unless you're very adventurous and experienced, the trip to the huts is more than enough for one day.

The spectacular Elk Mountains from Pearl Pass Road

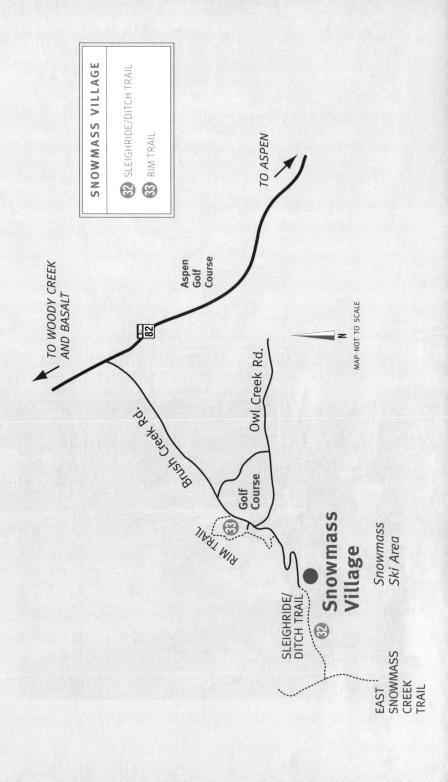

SNOWMASS VILLAGE

32 SLEIGHRIDE/DITCH TRAIL

33 RIM TRAIL

TO ASPEN

Aspen Golf Course

TO WOODY CREEK AND BASALT

82

Owl Creek Rd.

Brush Creek Rd.

N

MAP NOT TO SCALE

Golf Course

33 RIM TRAIL

SLEIGHRIDE/ DITCH TRAIL

32 Snowmass Village

Snowmass Ski Area

EAST SNOWMASS CREEK TRAIL

The focal point of cross-country skiing and snowshoeing in Snowmass Village is the Snowmass Cross-Country Ski and Snowshoe Center at the Snowmass Golf Course (described earlier in Route #7). The Sleighride/Ditch Trail leading from the Top of the Village is a popular close-in trail for hikers, skiers and snowshoers looking for a short pleasant tour, or a way to get to the East Snowmass Trail. The nearby Rim Trail is a steeper, more demanding route for hikers and snowshoers which leads onto a ridge overlooking Snowmass Village, Wildcat and the surrounding mountain peaks. Other short routes (not described here) weave around between the ski slopes. Snowmass Village also serves as the western terminus for the Government and Owl Creek trails from Aspen/Buttermilk (see routes #26 and #27).

Sleighride/Ditch Trail

MAPS: Aspen/Snowmass Outdoors, Basalt/Carbondale Outdoors, TI #128

DISTANCE: Sleighride Trail—1.5 miles roundtrip to Ditch Trail; Ditch Trail—3.5 miles roundtrip to the East Snowmass Trail

ELEVATION: 8,900–9,180 feet

ACCESS: From the Snowmass Village Mall (permit parking) walk up (or catch a shuttle) the Snowmelt Road to Top of the Village to the gate at the top of the road for the Sleighride Trail. For access directly to the Ditch Trail, take Divide Road from Brush Creek Road one mile to the Divide Parking lot (a permit is required to park here). The trail heads out of the end of the upper Divide Lot.

Comments

This easy, pleasant route is good for both skiers, snowshoers and hikers who want to head out from the Snowmass Village Mall area and get into the woods. The views of Mount Daly and the Snowmass Creek Valley are highlights of the trip. The Ditch Trail, which eventually takes you across the Campground portion of the ski area to the East Snowmass Creek Valley and the East Snowmass Trail (see Route #38), involves crossing several downhill ski slopes along the way. The trail is generally packed out to the Powderhorn ski slope. Beyond the slope, the trail may or may not be packed.

Route

From the top of Snowmelt Road, on the other side of the gate, take a right onto the wide, packed-out Sleighride Trail. After a pleasant level stretch through the aspen, you come out on Divide Drive where you walk across the road, up Pinion Drive through the parking lot to the end where a sign indicates the way to the Campground Lift. This is the start of the Ditch Trail.

Stay to the left on the trail which contours and crosses the

Campground ski slopes and passes under the Campground ski lift one-half mile from the parking lot. Continue through more woods with some great views out over the Snowmass Creek Valley until you come out to a bench on the Powderhorn ski slope with Mount Daly looming ahead. Head up Powderhorn against the downhill ski traffic for a couple hundred yards to a trail angling downhill into the woods on the right. Head through the woods on a traverse as a downhill brings you into the East Snowmass Creek Valley. Stay along the left side of the creek valley. Upon encountering a sign for the Ditch Trail (facing the other direction) drop down to the right across a small ditch and then straight down to East Snowmass Creek to a trailhead sign for the East Snowmass Trail and a wooden bridge crossing the creek. On the other side take a switchback up the hill to another sign at the intersection with the East Snowmass Trail coming up the other side of the creek. If you wish to explore more you can follow the East Snowmass Trail uphill to the left (usually unpacked) or downhill to the right (see Route #38). Retrace your route back to the trailhead.

Looking into Snowmass Creek Valley from the bottom of Powderhorn

Rim Trail

MAPS: Aspen/Snowmass Outdoors, Basalt/Carbondale Outdoors, TI #128

DISTANCE: 7 miles round trip, but can be shortened to 3.5 miles by dropping off a car at the end of Sinclair Road at the trail exit

ELEVATION: 8,550–9,250 feet

ACCESS: From the Snowmass Village Mall follow Brush Creek Road to a left at Divide Road; at the first street on the right (Deerfield Drive) the signed Rim Trail goes uphill from the intersection of the two roads. Park in a small plowed area for the Rim Trail on Brush Creek Road just past Deerfield Drive, or try to use the buses, walk, or get someone to drop you off and pick you up. The trail can also be accessed from the other end by taking Brush Creek Road to Sinclair Road which you follow to the end. The trail goes up the hill from Sinclair Road to the left. This is where you should drop off a vehicle for a one-way trip.

Comments

The Rim Trail, a great route for bikers and hikers in the summer, also provides a good snowshoe route in the winter. This trail offers the best opportunity in Snowmass Village to get away from the ski slopes and the development that infringes on many of the other local trails. The north section of the trail is closed from 9/15 to 6/21 due to it being a wildlife sensitive area, so only the south section up to Sinclair Road can be used in the winter. The Rim Trail follows a ridge high above Snowmass Village and has great panoramic views out over Snowmass Village and up and down the valley. The route is long, high up, somewhat isolated, and has steep dropoffs; so be careful, don't travel alone, and avoid this route in bad weather. The first section of the trail is usually packed out and is a favorite workout route for locals, but the middle section, and sometimes the end section, of the route is often untracked— allow plenty of time and use a car dropoff if possible to make it a one-way route. Or, if you don't have a lot of time, simply hike up to the top of the ridge, enjoy the views, and hike back down.

Route

From the sign at the beginning of the trail you will have to climb first through some aspen and then up the side of the hill, continuing on some sharp uphill switchbacks. This section is usually well packed out to the top of the ridge. At the top of the ridge follow the fenceline on the right. The route basically follows along the ridge with continuous good views of Snowmass Village, the Snowmass Ski Area, Capitol and Daly peaks and Snowmass Creek Valley. Avoid going left off the ridge onto private property. At just over two miles, a couple of switchbacks down the back takes you on a short traverse through the trees before you regain the ridge again. After the saddle between the subdivision on the right and Wildcat on the left, at 3 miles you come to a sign giving you the option of going up over the knob on the left or traversing around the front of the slope. Stay right on the easier traverse for the last one-half mile to Sinclair Road, which is as far as you can go on the trail during the winter. Either double back, or take the car you dropped off back around to your starting point.

Mount Daly and Capitol Peak from the Rim Trail

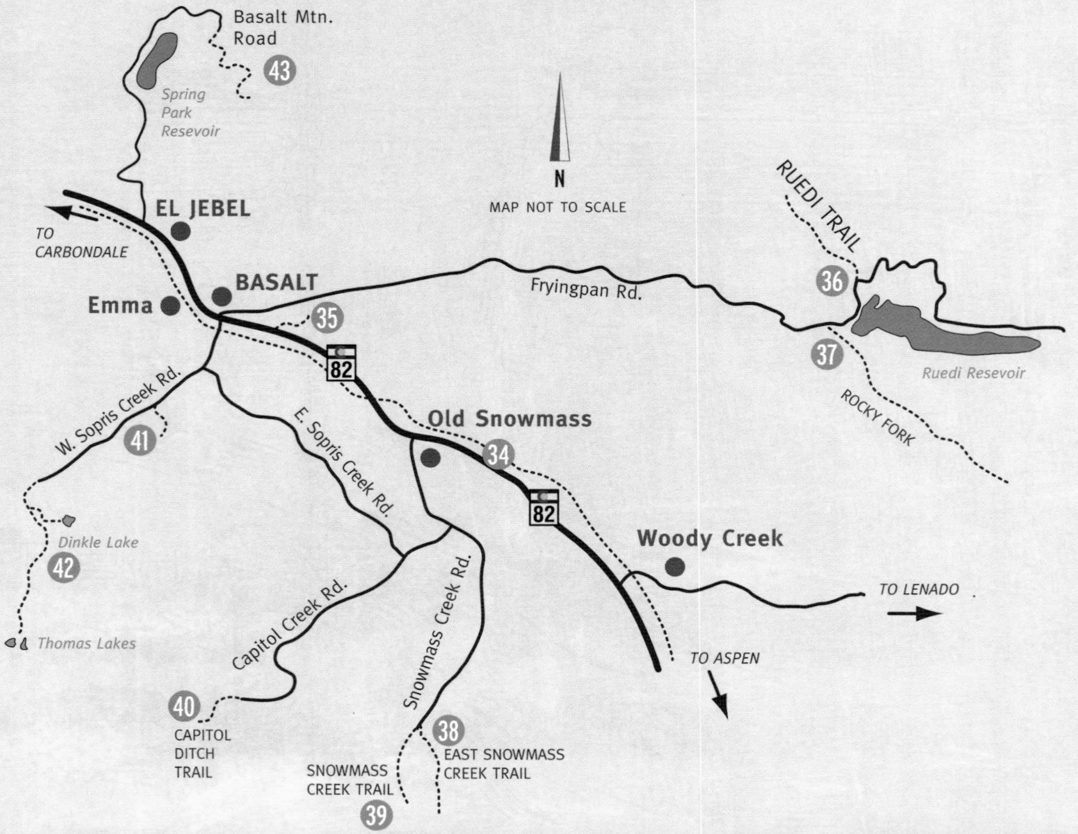

Ruedi Resevoir

RUEDI TRAIL **36**

37 ROCKY FORK

TO LENADO

Woody Creek

TO ASPEN

Fryingpan Rd.

N

MAP NOT TO SCALE

82

34

Old Snowmass

EAST SNOWMASS CREEK TRAIL

38

Snowmass Creek Rd.

35

82

BASALT

E. Sopris Creek Rd.

39 SNOWMASS CREEK TRAIL

Basalt Mtn. Road

43

Spring Park Reservoir

EL JEBEL

Capitol Creek Rd.

40 CAPITOL DITCH TRAIL

Emma

W. Sopris Creek Rd.

41

Dinkle Lake

42

Thomas Lakes

TO CARBONDALE

The midvalley area around Old Snowmass and Basalt provides access to a large variety of routes for winter use. Some of the more out-of-the-way and seldom used trails are up the Snowmass Creek, Capitol Creek and Fryingpan River valleys. Skiers and snowshoers will like the Snowmass Creek Trail, the Capitol Ditch Trail and the Thomas Lakes/Hay Park route, all of which lead into the surrounding wilderness. Steeper trails, more ideal for just snowshoers, include the Ruedi and Rocky Fork trails in the Fryingpan River Valley, the East Snowmass Trail and the West Sopris BLM Trail. For closer-in access, the popular local trails for hikers and dogs are the Rio Grande Trail and the Arbaney-Kittle Trail. Basalt Mountain Road, leading out of Missouri Heights, is especially popular with cross-country skiers, but is also good for snowshoeing and dog walking.

Rio Grande Trail – Basalt

MAP: Basalt/Carbondale Outdoors

DISTANCE: (west to east) Rock Bottom Ranch (closure gate) to Hooks Lane 1.75 miles, Hooks Lane to Emma Schoolhouse 1.45 miles, Emma Schoolhouse to Basalt High School 1.45 miles, Basalt High School to Trail Junction 2.3 miles, Trail Junction to Old Snowmass 1.1 miles, Old Snowmass Parking to Gerbaz Way 4.8 miles, Gerbaz Way to Woody Creek Road 2.3 miles (From Woody Creek Road to the Aspen Post Office is 7.7 miles)

ELEVATION: Rock Bottom Ranch 6,400 feet, Basalt High School 6,675 feet, Old Snowmass 6,870 feet, Woody Creek Road 7,365 feet

ACCESS: Hooks Lane, Emma Schoolhouse, Basalt High School, Old Snowmass, Woody Creek Road (all with trailhead parking); Gerbaz Way (parking up the road)

Comments

In midvalley the fairly level Rio Grande Trail, which follows the old Denver & Rio Grande railroad bed, stretches from Rock Bottom Ranch on Hook Spur Lane east all the way to Old Snowmass and beyond to Aspen. In summer the paved trail is used extensively by bikers, runners and walkers. In winter, when snow cover is sufficient, the trail is tracked for cross-country skiers, but it is also popular with hikers and snowshoers. The trail can be accessed from a number of points, some of which have parking areas just for the Rio Grande Trail. The land alongside the Rio Grande Trail in the Basalt area includes winter range for elk and deer, as well as active cattle-grazing ranches, so leash laws for dogs are strictly enforced. The section of trail from Rock Bottom Ranch west to Catherine Store Road is closed during the winter because of concerns for the winter habitat of wildlife.

Route

When snow cover is adequate follow the trail in either direction from one of the access points for an out-and-back tour. This part of the Rio Grande Trail is not always tracked out and doesn't get heavy use. When on cross-country skis remember that heading west is slightly downhill and heading east is slightly uphill. Obey leash laws.

Following the railroad grade near Basalt

35 Arbaney-Kittle Trail

MAPS: Basalt/Carbondale Outdoors, TI #143

DISTANCE: 3.5 miles roundtrip to the overlook

ELEVATION: 6,850–8,300 feet

ACCESS: Take Hwy. 82 toward Aspen from the main Basalt light (by the Texaco and roundabout) 1.4 miles to a left onto Bishop Road into Holland Hills. Take the first left onto Holland Hills Drive and go left up a short steep road (staying left of the dog kennels) to the trailhead parking.

Comments

This steep hike is very popular with hikers who are out for a good workout on this south-facing route. Many of the hikers also bring their dogs along for their exercise. The trail is always packed out, so snowshoes are not necessary, but some kind of cleats on your footwear are very helpful because of the steepness of the route. The spectacular sights from the top include Mount Sopris, Capitol Peak and Mount Daly, and other mountains of the Elk Mountains Range, plus the Roaring Fork and Fryingpan River valleys, and an overview of the town of Basalt. The normal turnaround point for most is the overlook into the Fryingpan River Valley, an elevation gain of almost 1,500 feet, but you can continue a little further along the ridge for a slightly longer trip. However, continuing along this ridge very far is strongly discouraged since this area is critical winter habitat for deer, elk and other wildlife.

Route

The trail heads quite steeply uphill from the parking lot on an obvious wide path through juniper, pine and sagebrush. You will be following a gulch as the trail climbs steadily, with only a few less steep spots to catch a slight breather. It usually takes around an hour or so to reach the obvious overlook at 8,300 feet elevation where you have good views of the Fryingpan River Valley, Basalt Mountain, and the Elk Mountains Ridge.

Ruedi Trail

MAP: TI #126

DISTANCE: 4–9+ miles roundtrip

ELEVATION: 7,980–9,160 feet (overlook)

ACCESS: From the intersection of Fryingpan Road (Midland Ave.) and Two Rivers Road in Basalt, drive up the paved Fryingpan Road. At 14.7 miles you will come to the Ruedi Creek Campgrounds and Boat Ramp. Go into the plowed out area on the right just beyond the sign to park. Walk up the Fryingpan Road another 100 yards to the signed trailhead in the woods on the left.

Comments

This seldom used trail, a snowshoer's hidden gem, offers the best views of Ruedi Reservoir and the central Fryingpan River Valley of any trail in the area. The trail passes through a variety of forest settings, the most spectacular of which are the tall straight pines. The route described here is out-and-back; just over 4 miles roundtrip takes you to the spectacular overlook out on Ruedi Reservoir and the surrounding mountains at the top of Red Hill. Beyond this point backcountry experience and a good map is recommended since the trail may not be packed or marked as it leads up to Red Table Mountain, eventually intersecting with Road 514 at 11,640 feet. Because of the good viewpoints across the Ruedi Reservoir along the way, the trail is also referred to as the Ruedi Overlook Trail. Skis are not practical on this route.

Route

Head up the trail through the forest as it takes long traversing switchbacks to an old road at one-half mile. Go right and then back left onto the trail. At about .8 miles you will start getting good views of Ruedi Reservoir. You then enter one of the beautiful stands of tall pine trees. After more switchbacks through stands of trees the trail reaches an overlook at 8,940 feet into the Rocky Fork drainage which stretches to the south below Ruedi Reservoir.

From here a long switchback through the woods takes you to the spectacular overlook at 2.1 miles and 9,160 feet at the top of Red Hill. Before you to the east lies a panorama of the Ruedi Reservoir, the Fryingpan River Valley, and the mountains in the distance. This is a good turnaround point.

For those exploring further, the trail levels off somewhat over the top of Red Hill and soon passes under power lines. Next comes a slow steady ascent, mostly via long switchbacks which follow the ridge in the forest, cutting from one side to the other. At 4.5 miles you reach a good viewpoint over Ruedi Reservoir, the surrounding area and the peaks in the distance. This is a good turnaround point for the longer snowshoe route. If time allows you can explore further along the ridge, but this is best done in summer during longer daylight hours and under easier hiking conditions.

Ruedi Reservoir and the upper Fryingpan Valley seen from the Ruedi Trail

Rocky Fork Trail

MAP: TI #126

DISTANCE: The length of the trip is only limited by snow conditions; eventually deep snow forces a turn-around, usually after about 2 miles into the trip

ELEVATION: 7,500–8,250+

ACCESS: From Basalt, drive 13 miles up the Fryingpan Road toward Ruedi Reservoir to a road angling down to the right. Park about 100 yards down the road near a bridge going across the river.

Comments

The Rocky Fork Trail, which is seldom followed in the winter, offers the snowshoer a beautiful winter adventure in the Fryingpan River Valley up a narrow canyon just below Ruedi Reservoir. Only the first half mile or so of the trail is suitable for skiers; beyond this point the narrowness and steepness of the trail preclude exploration on skis. The trail follows Rocky Fork Creek in a canyon surrounded by steep, avalanche-prone walls, so this route should only be followed during times of low avalanche conditions. The beginning portion of the trail may be somewhat packed out, but once the trail starts its climb in the woods expect to encounter some deep snow, so be prepared; it would be advisable to wear gaiters. Getting lost is not a problem—the trail follows the creek the entire way.

Route

Cross the bridge over the Fryingpan River and go left along the river. The trail starts out fairly flat, and follows the river as it bends south where the trail starts on an easy climb across from the Ruedi Dam. Here you enter the canyon which narrows with side walls rising steeply above. A little over one-half hour from the start, after continuing on the roadbed along the creek on an easy ascent, you come to a summer parking area and trailhead with a Forest Service small building. Ahead the steep walls signify prime avalanche conditions. Turn around if conditions warrant it. Just ahead the trail crosses over a small bridge, narrows, and climbs up steeply through a beautiful fir forest along the side of a steep slope. You soon encounter some spruce, and after 20 minutes or so the trail starts leveling out somewhat, surrounded by rocky walls. A little more climbing brings you to an open area (just under 2 miles into the hike) where you have better views of the canyon walls. The trail, however, heads back into the trees and continues to climb. You are now in the high country with deeper snow to contend with, and your turnaround point depends on your endurance and the snow conditions.

The beginning of the Rocky Fork Trail by the Fryingpan River

East Snowmass Trail

MAPS:	Basalt/Carbondale Outdoors, TI #128
DISTANCE:	3.2+ miles roundtrip
ELEVATION:	8,300–9,140+ feet
ACCESS:	Take Highway 82 to Old Snowmass (14 miles west of Aspen) and turn at the gas station south onto Snowmass Creek Road. Go 1.8 miles to a T-intersection and go left on Snowmass Creek Road. At 9.2 miles from this turn you will come to a winter end-of-the-road parking area just before the bridge. Park your car here, leaving room for the snowplow to turn around.

Comments

The East Snowmass Trail, a seldom used trail in the winter, can be accessed by snowshoers either via the Ditch Trail in Snowmass Village (see Route #32) or via the East Snowmass Trailhead at the end of Snowmass Creek Road. For a good uphill workout through the forest on an easy-to-follow route, even when it is unpacked, try starting at the East Snowmass Trailhead as described below. Be aware that the route will generally be unpacked and quite steep for the initial two-thirds mile up from the trailhead. Venturing beyond the trail junction at 9,140 feet may involve some route-finding and crossing avalanche paths. As always in the backcountry, travel with someone and be aware of potential avalanche danger.

Route

Cross the bridge on the plowed road over Snowmass Creek. In 200 yards, where the plowed road goes left to a private residence, stay straight on the unplowed, packed road for another 200 yards to a "T" where you go right on the track packed by dog sled teams. In 300 yards you will come to the East Snowmass Creek trailhead on the left.

Follow the trail past the sign on an uphill climb that soon steepens, using long switchbacks through the woods to climb the wooded mountainside. In two-thirds of a mile, at the top of the switchbacks, the route enters the Maroon Bells–Snowmass Wilderness, as indicated by a sign. From this point the route levels somewhat as it stays to the right above the East Snowmass Creek drainage. At 1.2 miles, after an elevation gain of over 800 feet, the trail comes to a junction, with a sign indicating that the East Snowmass Trail, Trail 1977, heads up to the right. (The trail going down to the left crosses the creek and connects with the Ditch Trail to Snowmass Village.) This is a good turnaround point, or you can continue up the East Snowmass Trail for further exploration if you have the energy.

Continuing up the East Snowmass Trail involves another mile of steady climbing (at times the trail may be hard to follow) before the way opens up and you can see the peaks ahead. Continuing on takes you through open areas and spruce stands in the middle of the valley. Be aware of avalanche conditions, and turn around and retrace your track when necessary.

The East Snowmass Trailhead

Snowmass Creek Trail

MAPS:	Basalt/Carbondale Outdoors, TI #128
DISTANCE:	Anywhere from 4–8 miles, depending on snow conditions and when you decide to turn around
ELEVATION:	8,300–8,700+ feet
ACCESS:	Take Highway 82 to Old Snowmass (14 miles west of Aspen) and turn at the gas station south onto Snowmass Creek Road. Go 1.8 miles to a T-intersection and go left on Snowmass Creek Road. At 9.2 miles from this turn you will come to a winter end-of-the-road parking area just before the bridge. Park your car here, leaving room for the snowplow to turn around.

Comments

This pleasant tour through the woods into the Snowmass Creek Valley takes the snowshoer or skier back into Wilderness where few people go in the winter. Snowshoeing is preferable, but cross-country skis also work on this trail. You may or may not find other tracks, so wear gaiters and expect to experience some deep snow. If the trail has not been tracked out from the trailhead, there may be some difficulty in following it, but it's worth the adventure. You can always make your own tracks and follow them back. What better way to see the backcountry in the winter!

Part of the route to the trailhead is used extensively by dogsled teams, so be aware of their approach and yield the right-of-way. Also be careful not to stray onto the ranch which is off to the side of the trail. The trail crosses a couple of avalanche paths, so check with the Forest Service on avalanche conditions before undertaking this trip. For the drive in, be aware that the upper part of Snowmass Creek Road can be snow-covered, and driving conditions can be bad after a snow. The road does eventually get plowed up to the creek where you will be starting.

Route

Cross the bridge over Snowmass Creek. In 200 yards, where the plowed road goes left to a private residence, stay straight on the unplowed, packed road for another 200 yards to a "T" where you go right on the track packed by dog sled teams. You will soon (300 yards) come to the East Snowmass Creek trailhead on the left (a possible snowshoe route, but quite steep—see Route #38). Continue past the trailhead for another .2 miles to a (summer) parking area for the Snowmass Creek Trail (Maroon-Snowmass Trail) with the trailhead on the left. Do not follow the dogsled tracks through the ranch, but head up into the aspens on the left at the sign for Trail #1975. After a short climb through the aspen you come to a Wilderness gate. From here the trail traverses on a slow climb and soon crosses the first avalanche path. Soon you're on a steady uphill climb, crossing another avalanche path. The trail soon picks up and follows an old irrigation ditch on a level traverse around the slope and above the meadows of the Snowmass Falls Ranch.

After passing another gate you can look across the valley, and down to the river and snow-covered beaver ponds below. You will traverse across more avalanche chutes and descend a little closer to the river, staying left to continue heading up the valley. At times the trail passes through the trees, at other times it is in the open with views of the peaks ahead. At about 2 miles past the first open area the trail starts a steep ascent through the aspen as it heads away from the creek. This is probably a good point to turn around because of avalanche danger.

The Snowmass Creek Valley

Capitol Ditch Trail

MAPS: Basalt/Carbondale Outdoors, TI #128

DISTANCE: 4–10 miles

ELEVATION: 8,490 (public parking)/
9,080 (end of plowed road)–9,500+

ACCESS: Take Highway 82 east from Basalt 3 miles, or west
from Aspen 14 miles to Old Snowmass and turn at
the gas station south onto Snowmass Creek Road.
After 1.8 miles, at the "T" in the road, turn right on
Capitol Creek Road and follow it for another 6.3 miles
to the large public parking area on the right. The road
is plowed for 1.2 miles beyond this point to the last
private residence, but the only possible place to park
is at the end of the plowed public road where there
is sometimes a plowed space for a car, but this is not
guaranteed. Do not go up any of the private roads.

Comments

The opportunity to visit one of the most beautiful areas in the
Maroon Bells–Snowmass Wilderness should not be passed up
just because it's winter. As described here, the route ascends
Capitol Creek Road to the Capitol Creek Trailhead and follows
the level Ditch Trail deep into the valley, giving the skier or
snowshoer spectacular views of Capitol Peak and Mt. Daly, the
magnificent Capitol Creek Valley and much of the surrounding
wilderness area (don't forget to bring a camera). In the winter
few people venture into this remote area which is so popular in
the summer, so be prepared to break trail. Lack of parking at
the start of the unplowed portion of Capitol Creek Road usually
requires a hike/ski of over a mile up the plowed portion of
the road at the start.

Route

Starting at public parking, hike or ski (if snow cover is adequate)
up the plowed road for 1.2 miles to where the plowed road angles
off to a private residence. Climb up onto the unplowed road and

continue your climb (skins might help) through the aspen trees. In three-quarters of a mile at 9,500 feet you reach the Capitol Creek trailhead where you have spectacular views into the Capitol Creek Valley and over to 14,300-foot Capitol Peak, Mount Daly, and other peaks of the Elk Range.

Continue straight through the parking lot beyond the trailhead to the signed trailhead for the Ditch Trail. The flat ditch trail goes to the left of the signs, following an old irrigation ditch. The first part of the trail traverses the side of the mountain in the open above the valley with continuing spectacular views and then goes in and out of the trees. The views never seem to cease and you can turn around at any point to retrace your steps back to the car.

A Capitol Peak view from the Ditch Trail

West Sopris BLM Trail

MAPS: Basalt/Carbondale Outdoors, TI #143

DISTANCE: 5 miles round trip

ELEVATION: 6,960–8,000 feet

ACCESS: From Highway 82, 1.5 miles west of Basalt, turn onto Emma Road and take an immediate left onto Sopris Creek Road. Go 1.1 miles and take a right onto West Sopris Creek Road. Go 1.0 miles to the green gate on the left. Find roadside parking.

Comments

This seldom used old road/cow trail accesses the hills and sagebrush flats high above West and East Sopris Creek roads. Snowshoes are the best option for this peaceful hike. Expect to break trail, especially after a new snowfall.

Route

Go through the green gate and follow the old road as it immediately drops and goes right to cross West Sopris Creek over a small plank bridge. From the creek the road switchbacks somewhat steeply up the West Sopris Creek valley wall for about .7 miles through scrub oak, bushes and sagebrush. As the road levels out in the sagebrush flats above the valley, you can see across into the East Sopris Creek drainage and beyond. Soon the trail climbs again, gradually curving to the right and ascending more steeply to the right of a side drainage, until it reaches a shoulder at 8,000 feet between a small knoll on the right and a hill on the left rising to 8,222 feet. Ahead lies property of Sopris Mountain Ranch. This is a good turnaround point, or you can hike up the hill on the left to add a little more elevation gain, and then retrace your steps back to the trailhead.

Thomas Lakes/Hay Park

MAPS: Basalt/Carbondale Outdoors, Glenwood/Carbondale Outdoors, TI #143

DISTANCE: 4 miles roundtrip to the Thomas Lakes Trailhead (8,660 feet), 11.5 miles roundtrip to Thomas Lakes

ELEVATION: 8,170–10,240 feet

ACCESS: About 1.5 miles west of the main Basalt light turn south from Highway 82 onto the road going to an immediate "T", the intersection of Emma Road and Sopris Creek Road. Go left on Sopris Creek Road; at 1.1 miles you will come to a "T" intersection, where East and West Sopris Creek roads split. Go right on West Sopris Creek Road for 6 miles to the top of the divide and park on the right, just across from a road heading south along a low ridge toward Mount Sopris.

Comments

This route for skiers and snowshoers follows a jeep trail which takes you to the foot of Mount Sopris. The views of the Roaring Fork Valley and Mount Sopris from this trail are unequaled from any other point in the area. The route is a good one for various goals which you can set your sight on—Dinkle Lake, Hay Park, Thomas Lakes, or just anywhere along the way. The first part of the route is usually packed by snowmobiles, but the latter part to Thomas Lakes is closed to snowmobiles and is often untracked, which can cause some difficult route-finding. But, since the lakes lie at the foot of Mount Sopris, heading toward the mountain will take you to your goal. The trip to the lakes gains over 2,000 feet in elevation, so allow plenty of time for the trip. Past the Thomas Lakes Trailhead skins are recommended for your skis, which is the preferred mode of travel along this route.

Route

From parking follow the snowmobile-packed Dinkle Lake Road as it climbs slowly for 2 miles toward Mount Sopris and the summer parking lot and trailhead for Thomas Lakes Trail. This can be a turnaround point for a pleasant 4-mile trip with an elevation gain of only 500 feet. Take time to enjoy the views of the valley and surrounding mountains. Dinkle Lake, if this is your destination, lies straight ahead down the road a little over one-quarter mile ahead.

The best route however, is to continue up the trail to the right past the trailhead toward Thomas Lakes, following a jeep road that climbs steadily on long switchbacks through the woods. Skiers should follow the road, but snowshoers may be able to cut some of the switchbacks by following steep tracks up through the woods. In just over a mile you will come to a small gate and open meadows with Mount Sopris standing out prominently ahead.

Follow the road as it contours left (it may be hard to follow in the open meadows) and then to the right to a wooden sign indicating a trail going off to the left to Hay Park. This can be a good destination if there are any tracks to follow. It is about 2.5 miles from this point through the trees to the spectacular views of the Elk Mountains Range from Hay Park.

If you prefer going to Thomas Lakes, stay on the main road past the Hay Park Trail intersection, heading west up a ridge to a windblown open area where you will head left into the trees toward Mount Sopris. A sign as you enter the woods indicates that no snowmobiles are allowed beyond this point. For the next 1.5 miles the hard-to-follow route continues in and out of the trees with gorgeous views of Mount Sopris ahead of you. Eventually you will reach the Thomas Lakes and the wilderness boundary sign. Take one last look at Mount Sopris from the lake and follow your tracks back.

43 Basalt Mountain Road

MAPS:	Basalt/Carbondale Outdoors, TI #143
DISTANCE:	4 miles round trip to the junction of Road 509 and Basalt Mountain Road; up to 9.5 miles round trip on Road 509; up to 14 miles or more round trip to the flats on top of Basalt Mountain via Basalt Mountain Road
ELEVATION:	7,550–8,000 feet (Road 509), 7,550 –9,600 feet (Basalt Mountain Road)
ACCESS:	From Highway 82 turn north at the light in El Jebel (between Basalt and Carbondale) onto El Jebel Road, which turns into Upper Cattle Creek Road. At 5.5 miles stay straight on Basalt Mountain Road. In one-quarter mile park at the winter closure gate.

Comments

Basalt Mountain Road offers cross-country skiers, snowshoers and hikers a beautiful route for a pleasant, easy route out of Missouri Heights and close to Basalt and El Jebel. In addition, the road provides access to Basalt Mountain and a number of possibilities for further winter exploration. Two miles in from the winter closure the skier or snowshoer has a choice of following Road 509 for another 2.75 miles to its end below the back of Basalt Mountain, or of climbing up Basalt Mountain Road around the west side of Basalt Mountain through a beautiful forest with an occasional overlook out onto the surrounding heights and valleys.

Route

From the winter closure gate ski/walk up Basalt Mountain Road to a cattle guard at .7 miles. At this point you can continue straight on Basalt Mountain Road or, just beyond the cattle guard, go down the roadcut that veers off to the right (the preferred route for skiers and snowshoers). After a short downhill the roadcut on the right gradually heads uphill through the scrub oak in a pleasant, quiet setting. In another mile this route goes through some trees and breaks into the open with some signs and the intersection of Road 509 and Basalt Mountain Road up ahead.

At the road intersection stay right to continue on Basalt Mountain Road on a steady uphill. Snowshoers can follow snowmobile and packed trails that shortcut the long switchbacks on the bottom half of the route. Skiers should stay on the road. Enjoy the views of Mount Sopris and the valley along the way, and retrace your route when you decide to turn around.

Staying left at the road intersection on Road 509 will soon take you, after a slight rise, on a gradual .5-mile downhill through the woods to a cabin on the left. At this point the road levels and slowly ascends around the backside of Basalt Mtn. to its end in another two miles. This road is seldom used in the winter and is a much quieter and more pleasant route than Basalt Mountain Road.

The alternate roadcut route to Basalt Mountain

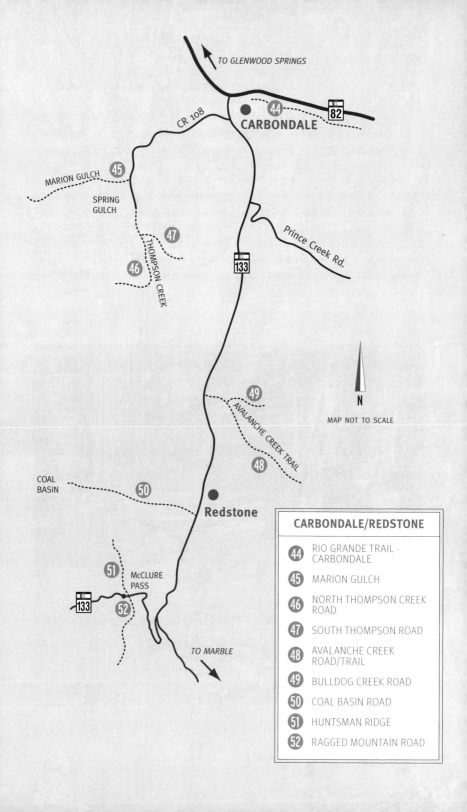

TO GLENWOOD SPRINGS

CR 108

44 CARBONDALE

82

MARION GULCH 45

SPRING GULCH

47

THOMPSON CREEK

46

Prince Creek Rd.

133

N

MAP NOT TO SCALE

49

AVALANCHE CREEK TRAIL

48

COAL BASIN 50

Redstone

51 McCLURE PASS

133

52

TO MARBLE

CARBONDALE/REDSTONE

44 RIO GRANDE TRAIL - CARBONDALE

45 MARION GULCH

46 NORTH THOMPSON CREEK ROAD

47 SOUTH THOMPSON ROAD

48 AVALANCHE CREEK ROAD/TRAIL

49 BULLDOG CREEK ROAD

50 COAL BASIN ROAD

51 HUNTSMAN RIDGE

52 RAGGED MOUNTAIN ROAD

The Rio Grande Trail in Carbondale is a favorite for hikers, dogs and cross-country skiers. However, Carbondale's prime winter sports area is Jerome Park to the west of town. Here, beyond the popular Spring Gulch Trail System, hikers, dogs, skiers and snowshoers find North Thompson Creek Road to be a favorite route. South Thompson Road and Marion Gulch both provide for a long-distance out-and-back for skiers and snowshoers. Between Carbondale and Redstone, Avalanche Creek Road/Trail is the favorite, with seldom-used Bulldog Creek Road being a hidden gem. In Redstone, Coal Basin Road is the most accessible route. Beyond Redstone, at McClure Pass, Huntsman Ridge and the Ragged Mountain Road give snowshoers and skiers a real backcountry experience.

44 Rio Grande Trail – Carbondale

MAPS: Basalt/Carbondale Outdoors, Glenwood/Carbondale Outdoors, TI #143

DISTANCE: 5.7 miles roundtrip

ELEVATION: 6,180–6,290

ACCESS: Follow Main Street in Carbondale to the east end of town and park. The snowpacked bike path heads east from the corner or Snowmass Drive, Main Street and Catherine Store Road. The trail can also be accessed from Catherine Store Road (CR 100) at the closure gate one-half mile south of Highway 82 just across the Roaring Fork River Bridge.

Comments

The Rio Grande Trail which extends from Aspen to Glenwood Springs is suitable for use in the winter from the east end of Carbondale on the south side of Catherine Store Road to a winter closure gate at the 90-degree turn by the bridge over the Roaring Fork River. Beyond this point to the east the trail is closed to all use up to Rock Bottom Ranch because of concerns for winter habitat for wildlife. This route is fairly level and is popular with skiers and walkers with their dogs. When snow cover is sufficient, the route is packed for skate skiing as well as being tracked for diagonal striding.

Route

When snow cover is adequate follow the Rio Grande Trail east along Catherine Store Road through the rural setting for up to 2.85 miles to the closure gate and turn around and retrace your route. Several driveways will have to be crossed which may require removal of skis when the driveways are plowed.

Marion Gulch

45

MAPS:	Glenwood/Carbondale Outdoors, TI #143.
DISTANCE:	5 miles round trip is the perfect trip and workout, but shorter and longer trips are good since this is an out-and-back route
ELEVATION:	7,950–9,150 (for the 5-mile out-and-back)
ACCESS:	Take Highway 133 to the light at Main Street in Carbondale (by the 7-11 store) and turn west on County Road 108 (Thompson Creek Road) at the light. Follow Thompson Creek Road 6.2 miles to a road on the right. Turn right and go .8 miles to the parking area for the trail.

Comments

This beautiful trail near the Spring Gulch Trail System west of Carbondale goes up a gulch into the high country and continues for miles over the mountains. The trail is a main snowmobile route, but its beauty is worth sharing with some occasional motorized traffic. If possible, use the trail during the week when there is little, if any, snowmobile traffic. Both skiers and snowshoers can use this route; however, the skiing gets more difficult as the route gets steeper higher up, and skins may be needed. For a long trip, make sure you have backcountry experience and use a good map.

Route

Follow the snowmobile-packed trail from the end of the parking lot through the aspen trees. A steady climb brings you to a gate at .5 miles. Three hundred yards beyond the gate the track drops to the left, gets narrower and follows the right side of Marion Creek. At one mile from the start a second gate and a sign mark the beginning of the National Forest. Just beyond the gate the route crosses to the other side of the creek as the trail narrows and winds back and forth in the firs and some aspen in the gulch. In one-quarter mile the trail crosses the creek again and takes a steady climb to a small clearing at 8,670 feet .4 miles up the trail. Beyond this point the trail will climb more steeply, so some skiers/snowshoers turn around here and complete their 3.3-mile roundtrip jaunt.

On the steep climb that follows to over 9,000 feet, skiers will probably have to use skins. At a little over 2 miles into the trip, at the top of the climb, the trail heads through the aspen trees and breaks into the open past another gate just under 2.5 miles. Here you can turn around or follow the snowmobile route into the broad, open expanses in the mountains ahead for as many miles as you have the energy. Watch the weather and retreat if necessary when bad weather approaches.

Top: The trail narrows through Marion Gulch
Bottom left: Descending into Marion Gulch from the west
Bottom right: Using the snowmobile track

North Thompson Creek Road

MAPS: Glenwood/Carbondale Outdoors, TI #143

DISTANCE: 4–7.5+ miles

ELEVATION: 7,700–7,900+ feet

ACCESS: Take Highway 133 to the light at Main Street in Carbondale (by the 7-11 store) and turn west on County Road 108 (Thompson Creek Road) at the light. Follow Thompson Creek Road for 7 miles to the end of the plowed road by the Spring Gulch Trail System and find parking.

Comments

Jerome Park is popular year-round with outdoor enthusiasts, and skiing or snowshoeing along North Thompson Creek Road beyond Spring Gulch provides a chance to enter a historic mining area with beautiful scenery. The first part of the route is frequented by walkers, skiers and snowshoers out for a brief workout, but the farther you go the more isolated it gets along the North Thompson Creek. On weekends you may encounter snowmobilers along this route, so plan accordingly.

Route

Follow the wide road south from the Spring Gulch parking area. In one-half mile the South Thompson Road (Road 305) angles down to the left, another possible route (see Route #47). Continue straight ahead on the main road on a gradual uphill. At about the 2-mile point the road starts curving to the right down toward the North Thompson Creek Valley. Mount Sopris stands out prominently to the left.

At 2.75 miles you pass over a cattle guard as the road takes a sharp bend to the right and continues to work its way down into the drainage. The next mile takes you above and to the right of North Thompson Creek. At 3.75 miles a blocked side road (the Air Tunnel Road) on the left leads to a mining reclamation area.

This junction is a good turnaround destination for a 7.5-mile trip. Continuing farther along North Thompson Creek Road usually involves breaking trail as the road stays above the creek on the right. Turn around at any point for a good long out-and-back tour.

Family day on North Thompson Creek Road

South Thompson Road

MAPS: Glenwood/Carbondale Outdoors, TI #143

DISTANCE: 6 miles roundtrip to the North Thompson Creek crossing; beyond here you can go as far as you are capable of

ELEVATION: 7,200–7,700 feet

ACCESS: Take Highway 133 to the light at Main Street in Carbondale (by the 7-11 store) and turn west on County Road 108 (Thompson Creek Road) at the light. Follow Thompson Creek Road for 7 miles to the end of the plowed road by the Spring Gulch Trail System and find parking.

Comments

This route from the Spring Gulch area in Jerome Park follows the South Thompson Road into part of the North Thompson Creek drainage and then into the historic Willow Park area west of Assignation Ridge. This road is seldom tracked out in the winter as it leads into a very isolated area with beautiful scenery. Both snowshoers and skiers will enjoy this route, but more distance can be covered on skis. The distance you can go in here is limited only by the hours in the day; it can be quite a backcountry experience if you continue on one of the many options off the road. Be sure to take a good map unless you are only going 4–6 miles. For your estimation of time, remember the last 3 miles of the return is uphill and will take longer.

Route

Continue straight on Thompson Creek Road for one-half mile (usually tracked by snowmobile) past Spring Gulch and bear left on a road (Road 305) angling down to the left into the North Thompson Creek drainage. From here the first 2.5 miles are a gradual downhill into the Thompson Creek valley, with mountain peaks in the distance and sagebrush, juniper, and scrub trees all around. The creek is in a gorge on your right; the road narrows as you head into the canyon and the side slopes steepen. After crossing North Thompson Creek at 3 miles (a good turnaround point), a gradual climb takes you to views of the rock formations in the area. The road soon drops down into Willow Park where you can turn around or continue following the road south, or bear right along Middle Thompson Creek. Both options involve a long day and a good map and sense of direction. Turn around at any point and follow your tracks back. You're probably going to encounter lots of snow along this route and will undoubtedly be packing your own trail.

Dropping into the North Thompson Creek drainage

Avalanche Creek Road/Trail

MAPS:	Basalt/Carbondale Outdoors, Glenwood/Carbondale Outdoors, TI #128
DISTANCE:	2.75 miles one way on the road to the end of the campground parking lot; from here you can continue on the trail and turn around at any point along the river
ELEVATION	6,750–7,350+ feet
ACCESS:	Take Highway 133 just over 12 miles south from Highway 82 or 5.5 miles north from the main entrance of Redstone to Road 310 on the east side of the Highway signed for Avalanche Creek. Take the bridge across the Crystal River and look for parking along the road without blocking private property. If no parking is available, park in a turnout on Highway 133 just north of the entrance to Avalanche Creek Road.

Comments

Avalanche Creek Road, located north of Redstone just off Highway 133, crosses Bulldog Creek and leads to a trail which heads into the wilderness and through the Avalanche Creek valley. The route is good for both snowshoers and skiers, but no dogs are allowed because of the critical winter habitat for bighorn sheep on the north side of the road.

The trail, which leads from the end of the road at Avalanche Campground, is popular in the summer but rarely used in the winter. The trail follows Avalanche Creek up a beautiful, steep-walled valley into the wilderness. However, beyond Avalanche Campground, the route will probably not by packed out, so you may have to break your own trail. The trail along Avalanche Creek in the wilderness area is easier to negotiate on snowshoes than on skis because of its narrowness and the traverses and short steep grades along the riverbank.

See Route #49 for a scenic side route off the Avalanche Creek Road along Bulldog Creek.

Route

Snowshoe/ski up the road past the alabaster mine and take note of the signs about wildlife winter habitat and the closure on the left (north) side of the road. You'll be heading on a very slight upgrade above the river into a beautiful valley with mountain peaks in the near distance. In less than a mile the road drops down close to the river in the trees. Follow the sign pointing to the campground, cross Bulldog Creek on a snowbridge at 1.7 miles, and at just over 2 miles you will enter the somewhat open area of the campground. At the far end of the loop in the campground is the Avalanche Creek Trail leading into the wilderness along the river in the trees. The trail follows the beautiful Avalanche Creek with the valley walls high above. At times the trail narrows and you may encounter some mud in spots if the snow level is low. Stay in the streambed area and above. Enjoy and turn around at any point.

Crossing the snowbridge over Bulldog Creek

Bulldog Creek Road

MAPS:	Basalt/Carbondale Outdoors, Glenwood/Carbondale Outdoors, TI #128
DISTANCE:	5.5 miles round trip; 2 miles round trip as a side trip off Avalanche Creek Road
ELEVATION:	6,750–7,750 feet
ACCESS:	Follow directions for Route #48 (Avalanche Creek Road) to the trailhead.

Comments

An old road off the Avalanche Creek Road leads up to an old mining operation in a narrow drainage and is rarely used by anyone in the winter. This 2-mile round trip excursion off the Avalanche Creek Road usually involves breaking trail, and even though the road isn't real evident, it's difficult to go astray since it follows the left side of Bulldog Creek the entire way. The historical setting of the mining operation and two tumble-down cabins make a good destination for a scenic and historic tour. This route can also be used as a side trip when doing Route #48 along Avalanche Creek.

Route

Snowshoe/ski up the road past the alabaster mine and take note of the signs about wildlife winter habitat and the closure on the left (north) side of the road. You'll be heading on a very slight upgrade above the river into a beautiful valley with mountain peaks in the distance. After about a mile the route drops down close to the river in the trees. Follow the sign pointing to the campground and, when nearing the Bulldog Creek crossing at 1.7 miles, go left about 20 yards before the creek on the old, indistinct roadbed which then stays to the left of the creek. Head through the scrub oak, staying to the left of the creek, as the way soon opens up.

At .5 miles the road heads up the bank to the left as it rises through the scrub oak and evergreens into the narrowing Bulldog Creek drainage at the base of the southern slopes of Mount Sopris.

At just under a mile the ruins of a large cabin (probably a mess hall or sleeping quarters for miners) appear next to the trail. Just beyond the cabin are the mining operation ruins on the hillside on the left, and then another smaller cabin on the left, beyond which is the end of the road, where you can get a good look up the Bulldog Creek drainage. This is your turnaround point for retracing your steps back to Avalanche Creek Road and the start of the route.

Top left: End of the trail Top right: Mining ruins along Bulldog Creek
Bottom: Ruins along the Bulldog Creek Road

Coal Basin Road

MAP: TI #128

DISTANCE: 6 miles round trip to the start of Coal Basin from the end of the plowed road

ELEVATION: 7,600–8,000 feet

ACCESS: The road heads west from the south end of the coke ovens directly across Highway 133 from the main entrance to Redstone 17 miles south of Carbondale. The first 1.4 miles is generally plowed. Parking at the plow turnaround is somewhat limited.

Comments

Directly across from Redstone, Coal Basin Road heads into an area with great winter recreational potential for skiing, cross-country skiing, snowshoeing, dogsledding, and other winter activities. This area, formerly Mid Continent property, lies about 4.5 miles up the road. The unplowed portion of the road before Coal Basin is ideal for a quiet ski or snowshoe through a scenic canyon. Coal Basin itself invites extended winter exploration.

Route

The first two miles from the end of the plowed road travels through a scenic, narrow canyon with steep walls and tall ice falls. The Braderich Creek Trailhead lies in the canyon one mile past the end of the plowed road. Beyond the canyon the route opens up. If weather conditions are favorable, continue into Coal Basin, explore, and enjoy the backcountry beauty.

Huntsman Ridge

MAP: TI #128

DISTANCE: 3–5 miles or more for a long day

ELEVATION: 8,750 –10,000+ feet

ACCESS: Take Highway 133 about 25 miles south from Carbondale (9 miles south from Redstone) to a parking area on the right about .2 miles before McClure Pass. If the parking area is not plowed, continue to the top of McClure Pass, park in the lot on the left, and walk down the road .2 miles to the signed Huntsman Ridge 517 Road.

Comments

Huntsman Ridge south of Carbondale by McClure Pass is one of the most scenic backcountry snowshoe/ski routes in the area. Backcountry skiers love to climb this route with skins and ski back down to the road. Snowshoers and cross-country skiers (with skins) can get a scenic tour up onto Huntsman Ridge and enjoy the views of the Crystal River Valley, Chair Mountain, Mount Sopris, and the surrounding mountain range. The climb through the trees is rewarding, the climb along the ridge is spectacular. This route is an out-and-back, so you can go as far as you have time. The minimum to get up onto and enjoy the ridge is 3 miles roundtrip, gaining about 1,300 feet. When continuing further along the ridge, stay on the ridge and avoid cornices and avalanche slopes. The route follows Huntsman Ridge Road from the trailhead up onto the ridge, but occasionally tracks are set which veer from the road to attain the ridge sooner.

Route

From the lower end of the parking lot for Huntsman Ridge, head to the trailhead sign or tracks going up to connect to the Huntsman Ridge Road. Continue along the road as it climbs steadily through the beautiful aspen trees. To the south you will have spectacular views of Chair Mountain and the Raggeds. Either continue on the road to the ridge, or you may find a track heading right off the road which accesses the ridge at 1.5 miles at about 10,000 feet overlooking Bears Gulch. From here you see the Crystal River Valley and Mount Sopris to the north. Follow the ridge as it heads northwest and then west on a slow, spectacular climb towards Huntsman Mountain. Turn around at any point and retrace your route back.

Top: *The winter wonderland on Huntsman Ridge*
Bottom: *Looking across to the Raggeds*

Ragged Mountain Road

MAP: TI #128

DISTANCE: Anywhere up to 10 miles round trip

ELEVATION: 8,750–9,850 feet

ACCESS: Take Highway 133 about 25 miles south from Carbondale (9 miles south from Redstone) to McClure Pass (8,755 feet in elevation) and park in the parking area on the left.

Comments

Ragged Mountain Road at McClure Pass is one of the most popular ski/snowshoe destinations in the Redstone area due to its usual good snow conditions, easy access from Highway 133 and spectacular views and scenery. The Road leads toward Chair Mountain and Ragged Peak; during the summer it is access to a few backcountry dwellings in the area. The route, which climbs through a peaceful forest up to a ridge, follows Ragged Mountain Road (Road 898) from the top of McClure Pass on Highway 133 for 5 miles to the end of the road on the ridge leading to Chair Mountain. While the first section is usually somewhat heavily traveled, the last section may involve breaking trail in deep snow, so be prepared with gaiters and either skis (preferred) or backcountry snowshoes if you plan to go the 5 miles to the end of the road.

Route

Take the road cut out of the end of the parking lot; the road is often packed by snowmobiles and/or other skiers and snowshoers. Continue on a gradual climb, initially on the Crystal River side of the ridge. Enjoy the spectacular views down the Crystal River Valley toward Marble. Soon the route crosses over to the Muddy Creek side of the ridge, continuing through the evergreens and aspen. At just under 3 miles, after an easy pleasant climb, you will come to an intersection with the Ragged Mountain Trail (#820) on the right just before a gate. Many use this as a turnaround point, but if you have the time, continue on for another two miles.

Follow the road cut which will probably be untracked, as it attains the top of the ridge leading to Chair Mountain above the Crystal River Valley. A gradual ascent of about two miles along the ridge brings you to a second gate where the road ends at about 9,850 feet elevation. Turn around here and retrace your steps back to the trailhead.

Chair Mountain and the Raggeds

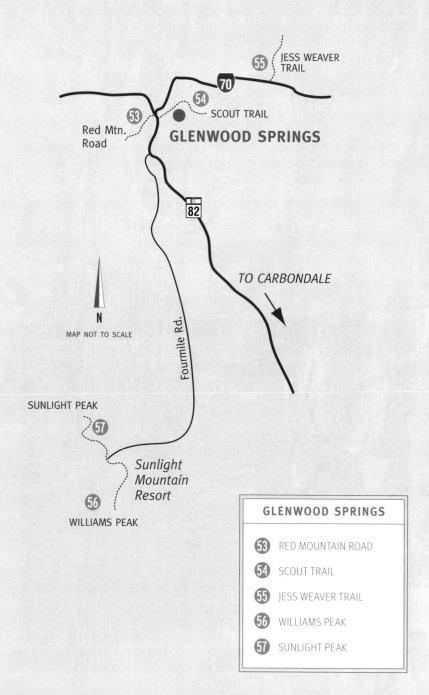

JESS WEAVER
TRAIL

70

53

54

SCOUT TRAIL

Red Mtn.
Road

GLENWOOD SPRINGS

82

TO CARBONDALE

N

MAP NOT TO SCALE

Fourmile Rd.

SUNLIGHT PEAK

57

Sunlight
Mountain
Resort

56

WILLIAMS PEAK

GLENWOOD SPRINGS
53 RED MOUNTAIN ROAD
54 SCOUT TRAIL
55 JESS WEAVER TRAIL
56 WILLIAMS PEAK
57 SUNLIGHT PEAK

lthough lower in elevation than the rest of the Roaring Fork Valley, Glenwood Springs has a number of outstanding ski/snowshoe trails ascending the surrounding mountains. Red Mountain Road, the most popular route for foot traffic, starts very close to the downtown area, passes through the site of the original Glenwood Springs ski area, and tops out on the ridge overlooking Glenwood. The Scout Trail on the east side of town gives snowshoers and hikers a chance to get high above Glenwood Canyon. In the canyon the Jess Weaver Trail, under good snow conditions, is a delight for snowshoers. In Glenwood's prime winter sports area around Sunlight Mountain Resort (where the Sunlight Mountain Resort Cross-Country Trails are located), Sunlight Peak gives hikers and snowshoers the chance to get up high, and Williams Peak provides a backcountry experience for snowshoeing, cross-country touring, and telemark and AT skiing.

Red Mountain Road

MAPS: Glenwood/Carbondale Outdoors, TI #123

DISTANCE: 6.5 miles round trip using the road; 4.5 miles round trip using the trail

ELEVATION: 5,870–7,500 feet

ACCESS: From Grand Ave. turn west on 8th Street, right on Pitkin Ave., left on 7th, cross the 8th Street bridge, right on Midland, left on Red Mountain Drive, right on 9th up the steep hill to the parking area and trailhead on the left.

Comments

Red Mountain Road is probably Glenwood Springs' most popular route for a good uphill outing. The route goes to an overlook high up the mountain by a large metal cross which is lit up during Christmas and Easter at night and can be seen from much of the lower valley around Glenwood. Much of the route has marvelous views of Glenwood Springs, Mount Sopris, the Roaring Fork Valley, and the Colorado and Roaring Fork rivers. Red Mountain Road used to be the access road for Glenwood Springs' original ski area, traces of which still remain. The trail crisscrossing and following the road has been named the Jeanne Golay Trail, dedicated to Jeanne Golay, an Olympic cyclist, who trained on this road and finished sixth in the 1992 Olympics in Barcelona. The road is plowed to give access to homes up the mountain, so most users of this route go up the road in boots or shoes, but snowshoers and hikers can also use this route by following the trail which crisscrosses the road. The road is also a good route to take in the evening after dark.

Route

If you wish to follow the road, go through the gate from the parking lot and stay on the plowed road as it winds uphill for 3 miles to a green gate closure on the right to private homes. Stay left on the main road for another 300 yards to the cross on the left overlooking Glenwood and the Roaring Fork Valley.

To follow the trail, go out of the end of the parking lot on the snow-packed trail to the right of the gate. You will soon cross the road and continue on the packed trail as it goes up steeply to the left of the water storage tank for a quarter mile through the scrub oak. At the top of the climb where the trail intersects the road stay left on the road and follow it to an overlook a mile from your start and pick up the trail again as it heads uphill away from the road. Continue following the trail as it makes several road crossings, cutting the switchbacks of the road, and gets steeper and steeper. When the trail becomes too steep, continue back on the road until you come to another viewpoint at a switchback (at 1.6 miles into the hike) and the marked trail takes off again from the road. The narrow trail continues along the front side of the mountain with beautiful views down onto Glenwood Springs and up the Roaring Fork Valley. The trail does a long switchback below the cross and heads back to intersect the road again. Stay left on the road for the last 100 yards to the cross on the left and the turnaround point.

The electric cross atop Red Mountain

Scout Trail

MAP: Glenwood/Carbondale Outdoors

DISTANCE: 2–4 miles round trip, or further for the explorer

ELEVATION: 5,900–7,000 feet

ACCESS: From Grand Avenue in Glenwood Springs take 8th Street east uphill to its end and find appropriate parking on the street.

Comments

The Scout Trail is a great opportunity for hikers and snowshoers to follow a historic trail starting right in Glenwood with spectacular views of Glenwood Canyon and town. The Scout Trail, which is hundreds of years old, was the Ute Indians route to the sacred "Yampah" Springs which now feeds the famous Hot Springs Pool. The narrow trail rises above the Glenwood Canyon toward Lookout Mountain and is mostly used by walkers and hikers for a quick trip and good workout close to Glenwood. However, snowshoers with some extra time can continue following the trail in the high scrub oak country toward Lookout Mountain. Beyond two miles out the trail is seldom packed.

Route

From the end of 8th Street head left up a driveway toward the trailhead sign and follow the trail steeply uphill to the right of the sign. The narrow trail winds around the front of the mountain and overlooks the Colorado River, providing spectacular views and lookout points. After 1.5 miles of winding above the river through the evergreen trees, juniper and scrub oak, the trail rises more steeply for a quarter mile up a ridge with views into both Glenwood Springs and Glenwood Canyon, then the route opens up and levels out somewhat as the towers on Lookout Mountain become visible up to the right. Just under 2 miles from the start you pass by an old abandoned pickup truck on the left side of the trail. Anywhere from here on is a good place to turn around as the route is usually not packed out at this point. Snowshoers can continue ahead and explore as time allows.

Jess Weaver Trail

MAPS: Glenwood/Carbondale Outdoors, TI #123

DISTANCE: Any distance up to 10 miles round trip

ELEVATION: 6,100 feet to 8,500 feet (5 miles up)

ACCESS: Take I-70 east from Glenwood Springs two miles to Exit 119 (No Name Exit). Exit, then take the first left to cross the bridge over I-70. Take this road north marked "No Outlet" .4 miles to trailhead parking on the left.

Comments

The Jess Weaver Trail (formerly No Name Trail) leads along No Name Creek from Glenwood Canyon up into the Flattops. When snow cover is adequate, this narrow trail is ideal for snowshoers looking to get some solitude in a scenic canyon setting. The snow-covered boulders and cascades in the creek between the canyon walls create a perfect setting for a "Winter Wonderland." Snowshoeing is the preferred method of travel up this trail since the steep, narrow and, at times, rocky trail which is seldom tracked out is difficult for skiing. Be prepared for slow going, good exercise and pure enjoyment. This route is truly a backcountry experience just off of the I-70 Interstate.

Route

Start by carrying your snowshoes. Walk 100 feet from the parking area up the road to a green gate. Walk around the gate on the left (the gate is usually closed) and continue up the road (which is usually plowed) on a steep uphill for .3 miles to the Glenwood Spring water system facility. Cross over the creek on the road and stay right as the road ends by a green facility building. At this point put on your snowshoes and head up the narrow trail from the end of the road along the left bank of the No Name Creek.

The trail follows to the left of the boulder-filled, cascading creek. A side creek on the left has to be crossed on a log used as a bridge. A tenth of a mile beyond milepost 1 is an overlook on the right into a small canyon. At this point veer left on the trail as it takes a couple of switchbacks up the hill on the left. Continue above the river through the scrub oak. After crossing one more side creek and regaining the river at 2 miles, the trail climbs more steeply and the river becomes more and more scenic with its snow-covered cascades. Just a little beyond milepost 3 the trail crosses a bridge. This is a good turnaround point (elevation 7,630 feet) for a 6.5 -mile roundtrip hike. Beyond this point the trail rises high above the creek, goes through some underbrush and eventually returns to the creek and a bridge with a plaque for Jess Weaver at mile 5, a good final turnaround point for a long snowshoe trip.

Top: *An Ice fall along the Jess Weaver Trail*
Bottom left: *Snowshoeing across a log*
Bottom right: *The water facility at the top of the road*

Williams Peak

MAPS: Glenwood/Carbondale Outdoors, TI #143, USGS quadrangle Cattle Creek. (Williams Peak is marked as peak 10079)

DISTANCE: Varies depending on the route; usually a mile or slightly more

ELEVATION: 8,720–10,100 feet

ACCESS: From 27th Street and Highway 82 in South Glenwood Springs turn west on 27th toward the river, cross the bridge, continue through the curve onto Midland Ave. 1.3 miles to the stop sign. Turn right onto Fourmile Road and drive 8.6 miles to Road 300 on the right, just one-half mile before Sunlight Mountain Resort. Drive up Road 300 for 2.6 miles to the Sunlight Snowmobile Tours parking area on the right. Either pay for parking at that lot, or park nearby on the road when adequate space is available.

Comments

Williams Peak, located at the west end of the Sunlight Mountain Resort ski area, is a great backcountry area for cross-country skiing and snowshoeing. The summit offers 360° views of the surrounding mountains and valleys, one of the best viewpoints in the whole area. There are no set routes for the ascent—telemark skiers skin up to the summit, usually via the northwestern ridge, and snowshoers head to the summit through the trees and open areas of the peak via any convenient route. Ski touring is also popular, and the lower slopes can be followed to Babish Gulch and the cross-country trails of Sunlight Mountain Resort. The north-facing treed slopes of Williams Peak offer ideal snow conditions for a true winter playground. This is an excellent introduction to backcountry conditions close to a road.

Route

Williams Peak rises above the road to the south and is easily accessed from along the road. To use the northwest ridge, where a track is usually set by skiers, go up Road 300 a couple of hundred feet past the entrance to the parking lot and look for a track heading up to the left. Generally you will be heading south to reach the ridge and then follow it southeast to the summit. On windy days the ridge can be quite windblown and cold, so a route more to the east in the trees would be a better call.

For a more protected and scenic route in the trees start off to the southeast from the road and gradually start swinging back to the south and then southwest to reach the summit. A topographic map and compass/altimeter would be a great aid until you have better learned the lay of the land.

Top: *The last part of the ascent up Williams Peak*
Bottom left: *Looking west into Fourmile Park from Williams Peak*
Lower right: *Happy snowshoers*

Sunlight Peak

MAPS: Glenwood/Carbondale Outdoors, TI #143

DISTANCE: 7 miles round trip

ELEVATION: 8,590–10,620 feet

ACCESS: From 27th Street and Highway 82 in South Glenwood Springs turn west on 27th toward the river, cross the bridge, continue for 1.3 miles to the stop sign. Turn right toward Sunlight Mountain Resort onto Fourmile Road and drive 8.6 miles to Road 300 on the right, just one-half mile before Sunlight Mountain Resort. Drive up Road 300 for 2.2 miles to a large parking area on the left. Park and walk back down Road 300 about one-tenth of a mile to Forest Road 318 angling up to the left.

Comments

Sunlight Peak, across from the Sunlight Mountain Resort, is the site of a number of radio, mobile and repeater communications towers. The peak, the highest in the immediate area, is serviced by a road which winds and climbs 2,000 feet through the aspen from the valley floor to the ridge which forms the peak. Snowshoers, hikers and skiers often use this route in the winter to get a good workout and to access spectacular views of the Sunlight Mountain Resort area, Fourmile Park, Mount Sopris and the many mountains of the nearby ranges. The road is generally packed by snowmobiles, but after a fresh snow skis with climbing skins can provide a good ascent and descent. The mostly south-facing route can be very warm and soft on a sunny day.

Route

Follow the fairly wide road as it climbs and winds up the south side of the mountain through the aspen, offering more and more views of the Sunlight Mountain Resort slopes, Williams Peak, Fourmile Park and the surrounding peaks. After about a mile some of the towers are visible straight ahead. After a little over 2.5 miles from the start the way opens up and it's possible to cut some of the switchbacks of the road by following a steep snowmobile route straight up the hill. You soon have the option of going right toward a couple of towers (at 10,470 feet) with a lookout point over the area to the south, or going up the ridge to the left to continue toward the top of Sunlight Peak (10,620 feet) and the maze of communications towers.

If you continue up to the left, you soon come to various arrays of towers and occasional views out on the surrounding area. Explore along the ridge and turn back when you have seen enough.

TOP: *Communications tower atop Sunlight Peak overlooking Sunlight Mountain Resort, Mt. Sopris and the Elk Range*
BOTTOM LEFT: *Hiking up the road through the aspens*
BOTTOM RIGHT: *Fourmile Park*

Index

Express Creek Road, 19, 81-82

Express Creek Valley, 81

F

Fanny Hill, 19

Finlandia, 34

Fiske, 31

Fiske, Billy, 30-31

Five Fingers, 63-64

Flattops, 138

Flynn, 30-31

Flynn, Tom, 30

Fourmile Park, 140-42

Fourmile Road, 20, 37-38, 139

Fryingpan River, 101-2

Fryingpan River Valley, 95, 98-102

Fryingpan Road, 99, 101

Funnel, 19

G

Ginny Lane, 34

Glades, 39

Glenwood Canyon, 133, 136, 138

Golay, Jeanne, 134

Golden Horn, 17

Goodwin Greene Hut, 81

Government Trail, 41, 59, 68-72, 89

Green Cabin, 19

Green Wilson Hut, 85, 87

Grottos, 43

Gwyn's High Alpine, 19

H

Hayden Peak, 57, 63-64, 66-67

Hay Park, 110-11

Hay Park Trail, 95, 111

Highball, 34

Highland Peak, 64

Highlands Bowl, 63-64, 66

Highlands Ridge, 65

High School Trail, 25

Holdens, 34

Horseshoe Lode, 63

Hunley Warming Hut, 30-31

Hunter Creek, 48-53

Hunter Creek Trail, 41, 49-52

Hunter Valley, 41, 49-53, 67

Hunter Valley Trail, 9, 41, 49-50

Huntsman Mountain, 129

Huntsman Ridge, 115, 128-29

Huntsman Ridge Road, 128

Hurricane Gulch, 65

I

Independence, 42-43

Independence Pass, 42, 44, 46, 66-67

Independence Pass Road, 9, 41-44

J

Jeanne Golay Trail, 134

Jerome Park, 9, 17, 23, 33 115, 119, 121

Jess Weaver Trail, 133, 137-38

Notes

Notes

Notes